NEW YORK

IN THE
NINETEENTH CENTURY

317 ENGRAVINGS FROM "HARPER'S WEEKLY"
AND OTHER CONTEMPORARY SOURCES

JOHN GRAFTON

SECOND EDITION

DOVER PUBLICATIONS, INC.

NEW YORK

Published in Canada by General Publishing Company, Ltd., 30 Lesmill Road, Don Mills, Toronto, Ontario.
Published in the United Kingdom by Constable and Company

New York in the Nineteenth Century: 317 Engravings from Harper's Weekly *and Other Contemporary Sources* is a new work, first published by Dover Publications, Inc., in 1977.

This second edition, published in 1980, contains a newly prepared index to artists and a general index.

DOVER *Pictorial Archive* SERIES

International Standard Book Number: 0-486-23516-5
Library of Congress Catalog Card Number: 77-73339

Manufactured in the United States of America
Dover Publications, Inc.
31 East 2nd Street
Mineola, N.Y. 11501

RUSH HOUR, 1890 (frontispiece). An 1890s version of the rush hour on the elevated in the rain. The appearance and dress of this crowd of commuters makes clear that the new elevated lines were used extensively by the city's prosperous middle and upper classes on the way to and from their businesses. (*Harper's Weekly*; February 8, 1890; T. de Thulstrup.)

INTRODUCTION

New York in the Nineteenth Century contains 317 views of New York life originally published in illustrated periodicals between the 1850s and the early 1890s. Selected from such publications as the short-lived *Illustrated News* (issued only in 1853) and from such immensely popular and long-lived journals as *Frank Leslie's Illustrated Newspaper* and, above all, *Harper's Weekly*, the engravings give a varied and balanced picture of New York during a crucial and fascinating period in the city's history. During these decades New York grew from a city of just over half a million people, settled almost entirely below 42nd Street, into the world's greatest metropolis. By the end of the century the Greater New York which we know today had finally come into being, a huge, teeming city of five boroughs and a growing population, drawn from all over the world, of over three million.

The 1850s were a decade marked for New Yorkers by a growing interest and pride in their own city, as seen, for example, in the creation of Central Park, as well as by increased concern with the world beyond the city, as evidenced by the excitement caused by the Crystal Palace exhibition and the Atlantic Cable celebrations. Badly torn apart during the Civil War, the city rebounded quickly when peace returned in 1865. The keynote of the succeeding part of the century was ever-continuing growth and northward development of streets until the whole of Manhattan Island was covered, and the present city of five boroughs was consolidated in 1898.

Many of the illustrations presented here reflect two of the principal themes that dominated the city during the period—that of the city as the nation's leading commercial center (with one of the world's finest ports and a busy financial district) and that of the city as the nation's leader in the arts, especially architecture. New York's position as the first city in America was probably solidified forever by the construction of two of the nineteenth century's Seven Wonders—the Brooklyn Bridge and the Statue of Liberty, both finished in the 1880s. These things set New York apart from other cities and helped to make and keep it the unique place it has always been, both in myth and in reality. The artists who documented these events surely believed that the New York they chronicled was in many ways itself the biggest news story of the century.

There was, however, another side to New York during the second half of the nineteenth century. Vast numbers of unskilled immigrants arrived daily and, finding limited opportunities, had nowhere else to go but the city's already crowded slums. This huge, permanent population of the poor and the hopeless was a problem with which the city did not even pretend to cope as the century wore on. New Yorkers in the nineteenth century were forever reading books such as James McCabe's *Lights and Shadows of New York Life* and Matthew Hale Smith's *Sunshine and Shadow in New York*, which set out to characterize graphically what seemed to their authors and to many others the dominant characteristic of the city during this whole period—the great contrasts which life in New York afforded between rich and poor, high life and low life, the mansions of Fifth Avenue and the dives of the Five Points. The reality of these contrasts comes through unmistakably in these illustrations. The inescapable fact is that the great city, with its brilliant architecture, its music and museums, its Coaching Club and its Wall Street, was also the city overrun by crime and disease, the city of tenements and sweatshops and homeless children who slept in the streets in the middle of winter. All that nineteenth-century life had to offer, good and bad, could, in short, be found in New York.

Very little of New York escaped the artists whose work is reproduced here. Only a few of these men went on, like Winslow Homer, to become great figures in the history of American art, but all of them were honest draftsmen, each of whom added something unique to our view of the city during these decades. Some were sentimental, some were satirical, but most were simply reporters. It should be mentioned that the kind of absolute accuracy we associate with news photography today is not to be expected here. It was not at all uncommon, for example, for pictures of great events to be drawn for *Harper's Weekly* and the other illustrated journals before they had occurred; this was simply the common practice of the day. Prejudices of a type that would be intolerable to the public today are also in evidence. Racial, ethnic and national stereotypes abound: the Irish are frequently portrayed as thugs, the Blacks as shiftless and lazy, the Jews as hook-nosed and crafty. Taking all this into account, however, there is still no question that the illustrations reproduced in this volume capture the look and ambiance of the city during the last half of the nineteenth century and do so with a charm and wit seldom matched by the news photographs of a later era.

It is worth considering that as we look at these pictures we see New York exactly as nineteenth-century New Yorkers saw it themselves as they sat down with their illustrated weeklies. They are arranged in this collection by broad, somewhat loose categories, but each engraving contains so much information on a variety of topics that these divisions should be regarded merely as convenient reference points and not as final or permanent labels.

By the time *Frank Leslie's* (1855) and *Harper's Weekly* (1857) began publication, printing technology had advanced to the point where large, fast steam-powered presses made possible the issuing of these popular journals in numbers undreamed of by publishers just a few decades before. Soon after its inception *Harper's Weekly* reached an average circulation of close to 100,000 copies per issue and *Frank Leslie's*, throughout the century, was not far behind. Despite the advances which made printing in such volume possible, the techniques of reproducing illustrations remained in theory similar to what they had been in the earliest days of printing. The technique of wood engraving used by *Harper's Weekly* and its many counterparts made possible the whole nineteenth-century phenomenon of illustrated journalism simply because it enabled pictures to be printed on the same press as was used for the type. Illustrations were drawn from a preliminary sketch in reverse on blocks of boxwood. (Occasionally the engravings were based on photographs. Several illustrations in this collection used as a basis photographs by George Rockwood, one of the most famous New York photographers of the period.) The part of the illustration which was to appear as white space was then cut away and the remaining raised lines took the ink and printed the picture. For larger pictures, several blocks of boxwood were joined together with screws. This technique, pioneered by Frank Leslie himself during his days as an engraver, enabled several engravers to work simultaneously on sections of a single large print; with this method, the huge double-page illustrations of historic events could be ready for the press within a few days of the completion of the original artist's sketch. When the separate sections of a large print were fitted together, engravers highly skilled in this particular branch of the art worked to make the lines from one section flow evenly into the next, and if this was well done it was impossible to tell from the finished print that it had been engraved in sections by different hands. (The job, however, was sometimes done poorly, and one can frequently see lines on these prints where the separate sections join unevenly.) As we might expect, competition was keen among the artists to secure the services of the best engravers as the look of the published picture depended as much on their skill as it did on that of the original artist. When the woodblocks were finished, they or stereotypes (and later in the century, electrotypes) made from them were fitted into forms containing the type for the rest of the page on which they were to appear and then printed like any other page of the journal.

Only in the 1880s did the means of reproducing halftone illustrations become available, but their quality was so poor that it was not until the 1890s that photomechanical techniques succeeded in making inroads in the territory that had belonged to the skilled artist. A few examples of pen drawings printed by such techniques are included here. After the early 1890s readers of *Harper's Weekly* were fated to see scenes of New York life presented to them in muddy halftones. It is not unreasonable to think that some readers may have looked back wistfully to the period when the publication's pages were filled with the outstanding wood engravings which are reproduced here.

CONTENTS

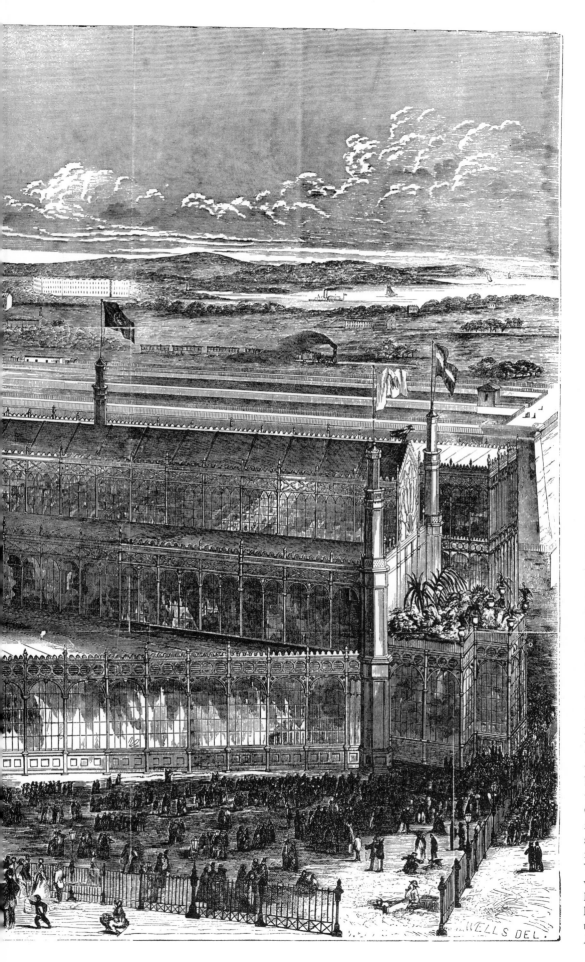

NEW YORK CRYSTAL PALACE, 1853. Modeled on London's Crystal Palace, which had been built in Hyde Park in 1851, the New York Crystal Palace opened on July 14, 1853. Designed by architects George Carstenson and Charles Geldemeister, the huge iron-and-glass building was shaped like a Greek cross 365 feet in diameter, with a dome at the center. The structure was built on Sixth Avenue between 40th and 42nd Streets (the site of today's Bryant Park), just behind the Croton Distributing Reservoir on Fifth Avenue (where the New York Public Library now stands). In 1853 this area was at the northern border of the built-up section of the city. The building originally housed the Exhibition of the Industry of All Nations. Great crowds turned out to view the imposing building and to see the thousands of exhibits of all kinds of manufactured goods from Europe and the Western Hemisphere. The exhibition was truly the first World's Fair to be held on the continent and was also the last such fair held in New York until the World's Fair of 1939. (*Illustrated News*; July 23, 1853; J. Wells.)

THE LATTING OBSERVATORY NEAR THE CRYSTAL PAL-
ACE, 1853. At the time of its construction in 1853, the Latting
Observatory was one of the most remarkable structures in New York
City. Named for Waring Latting, whose idea it was, the 350-foot-
high tower (the highest man-made structure in North America at
that time, taller in fact than the scale of this engraving would indi-
cate) overlooking the Crystal Palace, stood on the south side of 43rd

Street near Sixth Avenue. Built of timber braced with iron, the
observatory featured another novelty—a steam elevator which took
spectators to the various landings, which were equipped with tele-
scopes and maps and from which unparalleled views of the whole of
New York and much surrounding country could be seen. Unfortu-
nately, on August 30, 1856, the Observatory burned to the ground,
only three years after it opened. (*Illustrated News*; May 14, 1853.)

THE CRYSTAL PALACE FIRE, 1858. After the Exhibition of the Industry of All Nations closed, the Crystal Palace was used for various other displays. The building was thought to be fireproof, but on October 5, 1858, the wood and other combustible materials inside it caught fire. The high temperatures weakened the iron skeleton of the building and it collapsed. The entire structure was completely destroyed in little more than fifteen minutes. Firemen are seen here forcing their way through the crowd with their engine, but there was no chance that the primitive firefighting equipment of the period could be of any help. Incredibly, although 2000 people were inside when the fire started, no one was killed. Pieces of the Crystal Palace were soon being offered for sale as souvenirs of both the unique building and the catastrophic fire. (*Harper's Weekly*; October 16, 1858.)

THE ATLANTIC CABLE: THE CITY HALL FIRE, 1858. In the summer of 1858, on the third attempt, a telegraphic cable was successfully laid across the Atlantic Ocean, shortening the time needed to communicate with England and the Continent from several weeks to minutes. At the time it was considered one of the greatest achievements in the history of mankind and, in the waves of enthusiasm that rolled across America, many huge public celebrations were held

New York shared greatly in the Atlantic cable mania; on the night of August 17, the day after Queen Victoria and President Buchanan had exchanged messages of congratulation on the success of the new cable, such a large quantity of fireworks was set off from the roof of New York's City Hall that the building caught fire. The cupola and part of the roof were destroyed and had to be rebuilt, but no lives were lost. (*Harper's Weekly*; August 28, 1858.)

THE ATLANTIC CABLE: PARADE, 1858. Two weeks after the City Hall fire, a great parade was held along Broadway in which sailors from the *Niagara* and other ships involved in the laying of the cable marched to the cheers of citizens, who also cheered a coil of leftover cable which six horses pulled on a float. In this view we see some of the *Niagara's* men carrying a model of their ship past Mathew Brady's Daguerreotyping Salon. The day's festivities culminated in a celebration at the Crystal Palace in honor of the origi-nator of the project, Cyrus Field. Unhappily, the country's exaltation over the new miracle was short-lived. On September 4 the cable failed, unable to transmit further messages because of faulty insulation. The Civil War intervened, and it was eight years and one more unsuccessful attempt before all the problems were solved and a cable finally went into continuous operation between Europe and North America. (*Harper's Weekly*; September 11, 1858.)

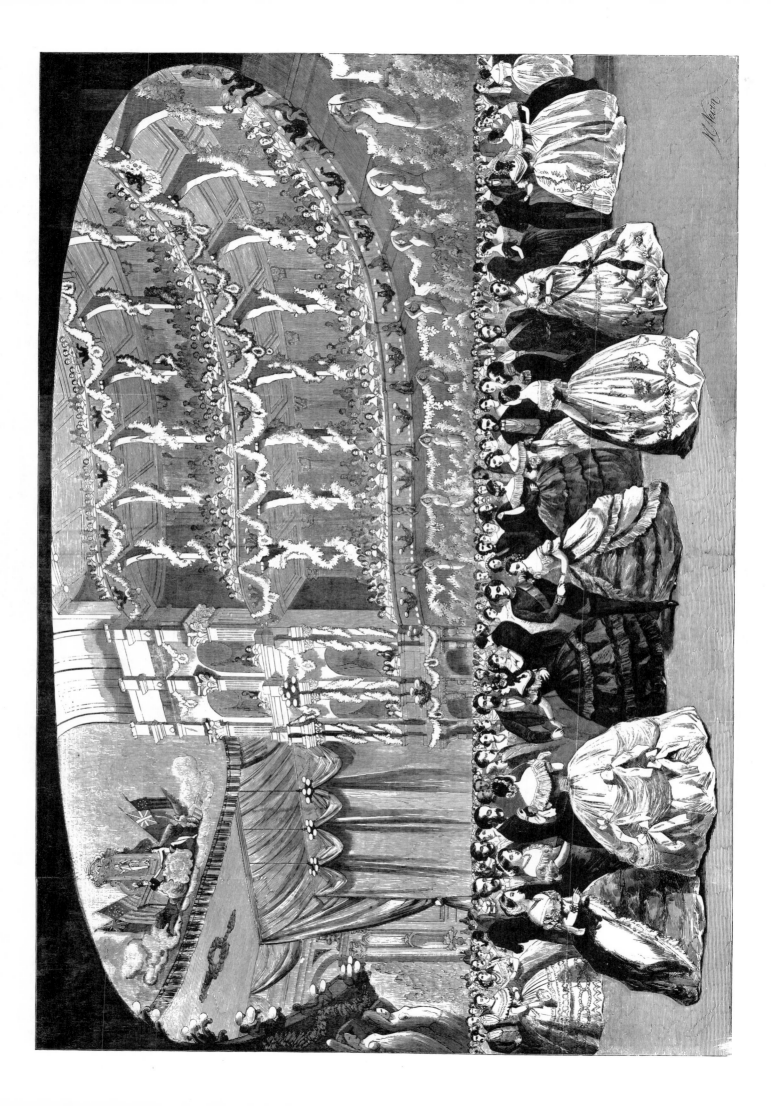

THE PRINCE OF WALES' VISIT, 1860 (Opposite). Vast enthusiasm greeted the Prince of Wales (later Edward VII) on his visit in the fall of 1860. A crowd of 300,000 lined Broadway to cheer as his coach drove from Bowling Green to the Fifth Avenue Hotel at 23rd Street, where he stayed with his retinue. He was escorted to all the sights of the city, entertained by the Mayor, and honored with a torchlight parade, complete with fireworks. 5000 of the city's volunteer firemen passed in review before the Prince, who was stationed on a balcony above the entrance to his hotel. The most memorable occasion during the Prince's visit was the grandest ball held in New York up to that time. On the evening of October 12, 1860, 4000 elegant New Yorkers, all of whom had been screened by a special committee which ruled on the socially eligible, filled the Academy of Music where a dance floor had been installed over the stage and orchestra. Hundreds of new gas lamps had been set up, and a temporary dining hall had been built in the backstage area. The nineteen-year-old Prince made a great impression on New York society as he

patiently danced with innumerable young women, and stayed almost until the end, leaving at 4:30 in the morning. It is certain that during his visit the Prince saw all there was to see and met all the great men there were to meet in the city. Legend even has it that, although he had yet to establish his reputation as a roué, on at least one occasion during his visit Queen Victoria's son escaped from his British chaperones long enough to enjoy a full evening at some of the city's less reputable resorts. (Harper's Weekly; October 20, 1860; J. McNevin.)
CIVIL WAR: MILITARY PREPARATIONS IN NEW YORK, 1861 (Above). Within weeks of the start of the Civil War in April, 1861, New York was serving as a staging area and embarkation point for Union troops being sent to the front. The top view is of the soldiers' camp on the Battery, where 2500 men were awaiting orders to march. The lower view shows the temporary barracks in City Hall Park, where 6000 soldiers were housed before heading South. (Harper's Weekly; May 11, 1861.)

CIVIL WAR: BROOKLYN NAVY YARD, 1861. *Harper's* reported that in 1860 fewer than 1000 men had been employed there; in the summer of 1861, when these views were published, over 2500 men were engaged in building new ships and repairing old ones for the Union Navy, and new workers were being welcomed daily. (*Harper's Weekly*; August 24, 1861.)

CIVIL WAR: THE LADIES AID ASSOCIATION FAIR, 1861. A Winslow Homer view of the fair held by the Ladies Aid Association at the City Assembly Rooms on Broadway to raise money for the aid of the city's poor, "especially that part of them," Harper's reported, "left destitute by the war." As the number of men in uniform makes clear, New York was now a wartime city with a different atmosphere than it had had a year before. The fair was a great success and a large sum was raised. (Harper's Weekly; December 28, 1861; Winslow Homer.)

CIVIL WAR: EXECUTION OF CAPTAIN GORDON, 1862 (Top). The hanging of Nathaniel P. Gordon, a captain of a slave-trading ship which had been captured by the United States Navy off the coast of Africa, took place in New York on February 21, 1862. Although slave trading had long been a capital crime, few offenders were prosecuted for it by the United States government before the start of the Civil War. Efforts had been made to have Captain Gordon's sentence commuted, but Lincoln had refused to consider these petitions. Diarist George Templeton Strong, applauding the President's firmness in this case, reported that the condemned man had in fact swallowed a near-fatal dose of strychnine just before his execution and it was all the doctors could do to keep him alive until he could be publicly hanged. (*Harper's Weekly*; March 8, 1862.) SUMTER MEETING IN UNION SQUARE, APRIL 11, 1863 (Bottom). The second anniversary of the attack on Fort Sumter was the occasion for this rally, seen here at the juncture of 14th Street and Fourth Avenue at the square's southeast corner. The focal point of the meeting is the equestrian statue of George Washington by Henry K. Brown and J. Q. A. Ward, standing on the site where it had been installed in 1856. At the end of the century the statue was moved to its present location in the center of the square's park. (*Harper's Weekly*; April 25, 1863.)

CIVIL WAR: THE DRAFT RIOTS, 1863. SACKING BROOKS' CLOTHING STORE (Top); CHARGE OF THE POLICE AT THE *TRIBUNE* OFFICE (Bottom). Throughout the Civil War, New York was a center for Northerners who opposed the Union cause in general and Lincoln in particular. Historians have ascribed this to the resentment felt by the city's huge immigrant population against freed slaves coming North to compete with them for laboring jobs. Moreover, many of these immigrants had come to America to escape military service in their native countries. This resentment against the war was kept alive by the city's Democratic politicians and anti-Lincoln press, and came to a head in July, 1863, when the new military draft, sponsored by Lincoln, was due to go into effect. The new draft law was especially unpopular among the lower classes in New York because of the provision which allowed a draftee to purchase the services of a substitute for $300—a sum far beyond the means of a common laborer, for whom it represented most of a year's income. The draft was scheduled to begin on Saturday, July 11. Fighting began the next day when mobs attacked the draft headquarters at Third Avenue and 46th Street. Over the next few days riots spread throughout the city. These are views of the rioters attacking Brooks Brothers' clothing store (then at Catherine and Cherry Streets) and the clash between the rioters and police at the *Tribune* building at Printing-House Square. Police, soldiers imported from the forts in the harbor and armed bands of civilians restored peace throughout the city by Thursday, the 16th. During the five days of rioting, perhaps 1200 people were killed while thousands more were injured. It is known that at least 18 blacks were lynched in various parts of the city while many more were reported as missing. (*Harper's Weekly*; August 1, 1863.)

CIVIL WAR: THE DRAFT RIOTS, 1863, BURNING OF THE COL-ORED ORPHAN ASYLUM. The asylum, which stood at Fifth Avenue and 43rd Street, came under attack on Monday, July 13. While a huge mob succeeded in sacking the building and setting it afire, hundreds of black children escaped through the back door. (*Harper's Weekly*; August 1, 1863.)

CIVIL WAR: A RECRUITING STATION IN CITY HALL PARK, 1864. About 110,000 volunteers from New York enlisted in the Union Army during the course of the war. (*Frank Leslie's*; March 19, 1864.)

CIVIL WAR: THE METROPOLITAN FAIR, 1864 (Opposite, Top). Beside the thousands of soldiers—both volunteers and draftees —who came from New York to join the Union Army, the city's greatest contribution to the cause was the Metropolitan or Sanitary Fair, opened on April 4, 1864 for the benefit of the United States Sanitary Commission. The buildings, erected especially for the occasion, stood on Union Square and along West 14th Street. The Commission had been founded in 1861 to raise funds for medical supplies for the Union Army, to staff field hospitals, to care for sick and wounded soldiers and to oversee and improve the generally deplorable health conditions under which an unprepared nation sent its soldiers to fight and under which it cared for them when they were wounded or fell ill. Before the work of the Commission had effect, field treatment of soldiers was at a rudimentary level. Overcrowding, disease, poor provisions and a general lack of care marked military encampments early in the war. Under difficulties and against great odds, the Commission succeeded in improving these conditions better than anyone could have expected. New Yorkers dominated the Commission. Frederick Law Olmsted, designer of Central Park, served as its general secretary; Henry W. Bellows, pastor of All Souls Unitarian Church, was its president. One tireless worker for the Commission throughout the war was New York lawyer George Templeton Strong, whose lengthy and readable diary, discovered and published only in the middle of the twentieth century, is one of the major sources for details of New York life in the middle of the nineteenth century, especially during the war years. (Harper's Weekly; April 23, 1864.) THE PICTURE GALLERY OF THE METROPOLITAN FAIR, 1864 (Opposite, Bottom). In this West 14th Street building of the Metropolitan Fair paintings which had been donated were sold to benefit the Sanitary Commission. Articles of every description were sold in the fair's various departments and by the time it closed over a million dollars had been raised. Similar fairs in other Northern cities helped to maintain the Commission throughout the War. (Harper's Weekly; April 16, 1864.) STOCK GAMBLING AT GALLAGHER'S, 1864 (Above). The war gave a great boost to speculation in stocks and prices rose considerably. There was so much activity that an enterprising gentleman named Gallagher opened this evening stock exchange at the Fifth Avenue Hotel to supplement daytime trading at the New York Stock Exchange. Eventually the bubble burst; financial scandals caused the directors of the New York Stock Exchange to announce that they would suspend any broker who participated at Gallagher's, and the new exchange disappeared as fast as it had sprung up. (Harper's Weekly; May 7, 1864.)

CIVIL WAR: THE END OF THE WAR, 1865. With Union armies in the South closing in on final victory, New York staged a huge triumphal procession on March 6, 1865 (two days after Lincoln's second inauguration). In this view part of the parade is seen passing the southern end of City Hall Park with the portico of St. Paul's Chapel on the left and a corner of Barnum's American Museum on the right. (*Harper's Weekly*, March 25, 1865.)

THE LINCOLN FUNERAL, APRIL 25, 1865. Robert E. Lee surrendered to Grant at the Appomattox Court House on April 9, 1865; on the 14th, Lincoln was assassinated in Washington. His funeral was held in Washington on the 19th and then the body began the slow journey by rail to Springfield, Illinois for burial. On April 24th, Lincoln's body lay in state at New York's City Hall while crowds filed by. On the 25th, this great procession accompanied Lincoln's coffin as it was drawn on this elaborate hearse up Broadway to the Hudson River depot from where it continued on the trip to Illinois. *Leslie's* claimed a million people witnessed the procession. (*Frank Leslie's*, May 13, 1865.)

THE BEECHER TRIAL, 1875. One of the most famous trials of nineteenth-century New York was held in Brooklyn (then a separate city), in 1875. The Rev. Henry Ward Beecher, seen here on the witness stand, was sued by his former literary protégé Theodore Tilton for having committed adultery with Tilton's wife. After several days of deliberation, the case ended in a hung jury, with the majority voting that the case against Beecher had not been proved. The judgment of most historians, however, is that he was guilty. (*Frank Leslie's*; April 17, 1875: J. N. Hyde.)

BROOKLYN BRIDGE. *Construction began on the Brooklyn Bridge early in 1870. For thirteen years New Yorkers waited impatiently as they watched the massive granite towers rise on each side of the East River; watched a seemingly flimsy wooden footpath being strung between the towers to enable workmen to create the four giant cables, each of which would be made up of thousands of individual wires, to hold the bridge itself; watched, finally, the wide roadway above the water take shape and reach completion. Even before construction began, however, the bridge's designer, John A. Roebling, was dead as the result of an accident on a Brooklyn ferry wharf. In 1872 Washington Roebling, the designer's son and the bridge's chief engineer, was permanently crippled by a case of the bends as he worked in one of the caissons below the water on the foundations of the bridge. Washington Roebling spent the next ten years supervising the construction of the bridge from his Brooklyn apartment, watching every activity through a telescope. Twenty workmen were killed before the bridge was finished. When the Brooklyn Bridge (at the time more often called the East River Bridge) was completed, it was the longest suspension span in the world. Its total length is 5989 feet—1595½ feet over the river; the rest comprising the length of the approaches on both sides. The official opening on May 24, 1883, was celebrated with speeches by many dignitaries and the attendance of President Chester Alan Arthur. On the following day, the first full day on which the bridge was open to the public, over 150,000 walked across. The only event to mar these early days came on May 31, when there was a panic when the bridge was crowded by sightseers. The incident could not, however, dampen the enthusiasm of New Yorkers for what they considered a new wonder, the greatest technological achievement in the city's, if not the world's, history, an accomplishment that seemed to contemporaries to exemplify the greatness of the age in which they lived.*

CABLE ANCHORAGE, 1883. The anchorage of the giant cables of the Brooklyn Bridge on the Brooklyn side seen while work on the piers is still going on. (*Harper's Weekly*; May 26, 1883.)

BROOKLYN BRIDGE: DEMOLITION FOR THE NEW YORK APPROACH, 1877 (Opposite). The contrast between the old city and the new is striking as workmen demolish buildings for the approach to the New York side of the Brooklyn Bridge—its mammoth tower already dwarfing the old buildings and narrow streets of the East River waterfront below. (*Harper's Weekly*; November 24, 1877; W. P. Snyder.) THE TEMPORARY FOOTPATH, 1877 (Above). By February, 1877, the wooden footpath illustrated here had been completed and New York had, in a sense, a bridge between Brooklyn and Manhattan. This view is from the tower on the Brooklyn side—another footpath led from the anchorage of the bridge up to the pier itself. The purpose of the footpath, which was strung above where the roadway would be, was to let the workmen reach the cradles (seen branching off from the footpath at intervals) where they would work on the cables for the bridge. The wooden footpath became something of a phenomenon in its own right. Walking across it was a popular pastime and since the men in charge of the bridge didn't object to having tourists underfoot, in a few months two or three thousand people had made the trip across. This somewhat placid engraving doesn't give an accurate picture of the effects of the wind high over the East River and, although there was very little to prevent one from falling off, miraculously enough there were no accidents; occasionally a sightseer became dizzy or immobilized by fear and had to be led back off. One lady applied for permission to ride a horse across, but was refused. From the background of what is one of the earliest panoramas of the city sketched from so high a vantage point, we get an idea of the relative height of the bridge when compared to the city's other structures, and a good picture of the highly developed waterfront along the East River on the Manhattan side. By this time lower Manhattan had completely made the transition from being a residential to a commercial center. (*Frank Leslie's*; June 16, 1877; C.E.H. Bonwill.)

BROOKLYN BRIDGE: THE FOOTPATH, 1877. A view of the wooden pathway leading up to the Brooklyn Tower of the great bridge. (*Harper's Weekly*; March 31, 1877; Schell & Hogan.)

BRIDGE TRAFFIC, 1883. "It so happens that the work which is likely to be our most durable monument, and which is likely to convey some knowledge of us to the most remote posterity, is a work of bare utility; not a shrine, not a fortress, not a palace, but a bridge." So wrote Montgomery Schuyler in *Harper's* as the great bridge opened in May, 1883—an event surely without parallel in the previous history of the city. This view makes clear the great lengths of the approaches to the bridge even as compared to the length of the span over the water. Five roads side by side—two for horse-drawn vehicles, one for pedestrians and two for trains—give an idea of the size of the bridge. (*Harper's Weekly*; May 26, 1883.)

BROOKLYN BRIDGE: THE BROOKLYN ENTRANCE, 1883. The great crowd pressing toward the vast entrance to the bridge's Brooklyn side dem- onstrates the enthusiasm felt by New Yorkers and Brooklynites for the city's newest construction. (*Harper's Weekly*; May 26, 1883; Schell & Hogan.)

THE BROOKLYN BRIDGE: OPENING CEREMONIES, 1883. President Chester Alan Arthur and his party as they walked across the Brooklyn Bridge as part of the opening ceremonies on May 24. (*Harper's Weekly*; June 2, 1883; Schell & Hogan.)

BROOKLYN BRIDGE: TRAINS, 1883 (Opposite, Top). A view of the passenger trains stationed on the bridge as *Harper's* envisioned them a month after the bridge opened. They went into operation in September (*Harper's Weekly*; June 16, 1883; Harry Ogden.) OPENING CEREMONIES, 1883 (Opposite, Bottom). A view of the Brooklyn side, partially hidden by smoke from the fireworks of the great celebration. The structure on the left is the terminus of the Fulton Street Ferry, built in 1871. The construction of the bridge heralded the end of the ferry. Although its service went into rapid decline, it did not cease operation entirely until 1924. (*Harper's Weekly*; June 2, 1883; Charles Gra-

ham.) THE PANIC OF MAY 30, 1883 (Above). A week after its opening, the bridge was being inspected by crowds of people enjoying the Memorial Day holiday. A woman lost her footing and fell on a short staircase that led to the foot-path on the New York side. Hearing her screams, thousands of people pushed closer, most just wanting to see what had happened. Others, however, created a panic by spreading the word that the commotion was being caused by the collapse of the bridge. Fear spread through the crowd quickly, and in the ensuing stampede a dozen people were killed and many more were injured. (*Frank Leslie's*; June 9, 1883.)

BROOKLYN BRIDGE: GENERAL
VIEW, 1883. The bridge from the
Brooklyn side, drawn just after it
opened. (*Harper's Weekly*; May 26,
1883; Charles Graham from sketches
and photographs by Gubelman.)

BROOKLYN BRIDGE: CROSSING IN A STORM, 1887. Even in the foul weather and high winds of a heavy early winter rainstorm, the never-ending stream of New Yorkers and tourists couldn't resist the temptation to walk across the new wonder in the years immediately following its opening. (*Harper's Weekly*; November 5, 1887; T. de Thulstrup.)

ODLUM'S JUMP OFF THE BROOKLYN BRIDGE, 1885. A reconstruction of the first famous jump off the Brooklyn Bridge, the leap by Robert E. Odlum, on a bet, on May 19, 1885. Although the police were on the alert to prevent Odlum's well-advertised jump, he outmaneuvered them by having a friend named James Haggert drive up to the bridge in swimming costume and attempt to reach the railing. As the officers surrounded Haggert, Odlum, waiting nearby incognito, threw off his overcoat and went over the side. He was picked up by one of the boats below but died of internal hemorrhaging 45 minutes later. Several people made the attempt to jump off the bridge and survive during the first few years after it opened and a few even lived to tell about it. (It now seems unlikely that the famous Steve Brodie, who made a career out of being thought to have been the first to make the jump and survive, actually ever jumped at all.) By the turn of the century this minor craze had subsided. (*Frank Leslie's*; May 30, 1885.)

STATUE OF LIBERTY: PROJECTED VIEW, 1875 (Opposite). To produce this engraving of the proposed Statue of Liberty before it was actually built, *Harper's* referred to photographs of sculptor Frédéric Auguste Bartholdi's model, which accurately depicted what the full-size one would look like, and superimposed it on a view of New York harbor seen from an imaginary vantage point. When this illustration was published in 1875 it was still hoped that the statue would be completed the following year to celebrate the American Centennial. Another ten years had to pass, however, before American citizenry donated the funds to build the pedestal (the French had paid for the statue itself more readily). Designed by Richard Morris Hunt, the actual pedestal does not resemble that shown here. The statue, when put in place, did not face out to sea as the artist envisaged here, but has her back to New Jersey (left). (*Harper's Weekly*; November 27, 1875.) CONSTRUCTION, 1885 (Above, Left). Workmen on Bedloe's Island putting the finishing touches on parts of the Statue of Liberty as the statue was in the process of being assembled. (*Frank Leslie's*; October 17, 1885.) CONSTRUCTION, 1886 (Above, Right). An unusual view of the interior of the upper portion of the Statue of Liberty as it was being assembled. Directions for the workmen may be seen written in French on the various parts of the mammoth sculpture. The statue's framework was designed by Gustave Eiffel, most famous for the Eiffel Tower, which he created for the Paris Exposition of 1889. (*Frank Leslie's*; October 23, 1886.)

BLIZZARD OF 1888: UNION SQUARE (Top) AND UPTOWN STREET (Bottom). Two views depicting scenes during and after the blizzard. Between March 12 and March 14, 20.9 inches of snow fell on New York, totally paralyzing the city. The storm severely damaged telephone and telegraph wires and plans were speeded up to install all such wires underground. In a relatively short time this characteristic feature of nineteenth-century life disappeared from New York's streets. The blizzard remained the worst in the city's history until December 26–27, 1947, when a new record for snowfall in New York was set with an accumulation of 25.8 inches. (*Harper's Weekly*; March 24, 1888; top by Otto Stark, bottom by Charles Parsons.)

MAY DAY, 1859. From the days of Dutch New York it was customary, if one was moving, to move on the first of May. By the middle of the nineteenth century, when *Harper's* published this satirical drawing, "May-Day In the City" by Alfred Fredericks, it was not only customary but fashionable. *Harper's* commented, "It has long been an axiom that food and rest are out of the question on May-Day in this city. Every one is moving; no one has a house; every one is miserable except the licensed cartmen, who are in their seventh heaven, and make $25 a day easily at this season, and the boys, who are blissful at the prospect of excitement, noise, breakages, mischief, and leakages." From contemporary accounts this scene was repeated a thousand times each May. (*Harper's Weekly*; April 30, 1859; Alfred Fredericks.)

NEW YEAR'S DAY, 1868. During the nineteenth century New York holiday customs were rigidly defined by long-accepted convention. Christmas
was a day spent always entirely with one's family but on New Year's Day
gentlemen made the rounds of the city, paying social calls on as many of
their friends and acquaintances as possible in a single day—often a hundred
or more—while the women remained at home to receive callers. *Harper's*
printed this illustration as being representative of a typical upper-class drawing room in New York on New Year's Day. (*Harper's Weekly*; January 4,
1868.)

THE RUSH FOR THE COUNTRY, 1868. The summer of 1868 was, according to *Harper's*, the hottest since 1824. The heat was blamed for 246 deaths during six days in July alone and doubtless caused many more that were unreported. "The result of the 'torrid term' has been to drive every body to the country or the Morgue," reported *Harper's*. William Ludwell Sheppard sketched this scene at the ticket office of a city railroad depot as New Yorkers, still heavily dressed for propriety's sake, pushed and shoved their way for tickets and trains to the country and relief from the heat. (*Harper's Weekly*, August 1, 1868; W. L. Sheppard.)

AUCTION OF HOME FURNISHINGS, 1870. The post-Civil War years saw no change in the fashionable New York custom of moving frequently. Every year the weeks around the first of May, the traditional moving day, saw many scenes such as this, an auction in a private home of old furnishings no longer needed. (*Harper's Weekly*; April 30, 1870; W. L. Sheppard.)

A DOWNTOWN LUNCHROOM, 1888. A lunch-room in Manhattan's downtown business district and not a woman in sight! (*Harper's Weekly;* September 8, 1888; T. de Thulstrup.)

CULINARY DEMONSTRATION, 1882 (Above). A mixed crowd watches an 1880s version of the short-order cook prepare pancakes in the window of a restaurant. (*Frank Leslie's*; March 25, 1882; J. N. Hyde.) A BEER HALL IN THE BOWERY, 1877 (Opposite, Top). One of the many German Beer Halls in The Bowery in 1877, complete with cuspidors and orchestra. Such establishments often had their own breweries in nearby buildings. (*The* [London] *Graphic*; February 10, 1877; J. R. Brown.) THE LAWYERS CLUB, 1887 (Opposite, Bottom). A gentlemen's club in the 1880s—in this case one of the dining rooms of the Lawyers Club, incorporated in 1887, which had its rooms in the Equitable Life Assurance Society Building at 120 Broadway. (*Harper's Weekly*; November 26, 1887.)

ST. PATRICK'S CATHEDRAL, 1869. An engraving made from architect James Renwick Jr.'s plans for St. Patrick's Cathedral, built on the east side of Fifth Avenue between 50th and 51st Streets. The cornerstone had been laid in July, 1858, but by the time this sketch was published the walls were only 50 feet high and it was expected that the building, which *Harper's* reported would be the largest ec-clesiastical edifice in America, would not be finished for several years. The building itself was completed and dedicated in 1879 while the spires, 330 feet tall, were finished in 1888. An error of scale in this engraving makes Fifth Avenue seem much wider than it actually is. (*Harper's Weekly*; December 18, 1869.)

TEMPLE EMANU-EL, 1868. Built at a cost of $800,000 in 1866–68 on the northeast corner of Fifth Avenue and 43rd Street, Temple Emanu-El was one of the most striking architectural monuments of the city. Designed by Leopold Eidlitz in collaboration with Henry Fernbach, the Moorish temple, capped by twin towers, held a congregation of 1800 with an additional 500 seats in the gallery. This midtown section of Fifth Avenue developed quickly and around the turn of the century it was transformed from a residential to a commercial area. Emanu-El was demolished in 1927, its immensely valuable site being used for stores and offices. In 1930 a new Temple Emanu-El was dedicated farther up Fifth Avenue at 65th Street. (*Harper's Weekly*; November 14, 1868; from a photograph by Lockwood.)

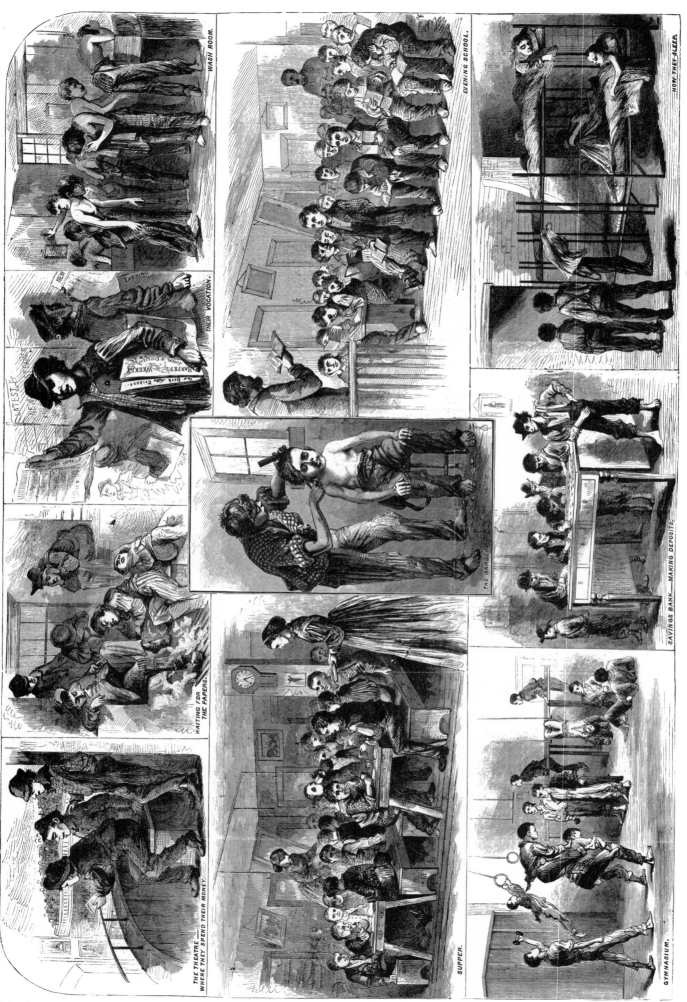

THE NEWSBOYS' LODGING-HOUSE, 1867. There were thousands of newsboys in New York in the nineteenth century, a great many of whom were homeless orphans, and one of the city's most notable charities was the Newsboys' Lodging-House above the *Sun* offices in Fulton Street. The Lodging-House was established by the Children's Aid Society in 1854 and provided a place where newsboys could live while they pursued their trade and received, in the evenings, a rudimentary education. As the newsboys earned money during the day, they were charged a nominal amount for their upkeep—four cents a meal and five cents a night for a bed in 1867. (*Harper's Weekly*, May 18, 1867; C. G. Bush.)

NEWSBOYS AND PAWNSHOP, 1871. *Harper's* frequently drew attention to the great contrasts—often expressed in moral terms—which New York life offered the sensitive observer. Newsboys could be divided between loafers such as those pictured here, who spent the time between the rush for the morning papers and the appearance of the evening editions by pitching pennies, and those who, like Horatio Alger heroes, used their spare time industriously by doing more work such as shining shoes for extra money. A similar contrast was to be drawn from the interior of a pawnshop, where unfortunates who pawned cherished articles to feed their children rubbed elbows with thieves who pawned stolen goods to buy liquor. (*Harper's Weekly*; August 12, 1871; top by W. S. L. Jewett; bottom by W. L. Sheppard.)

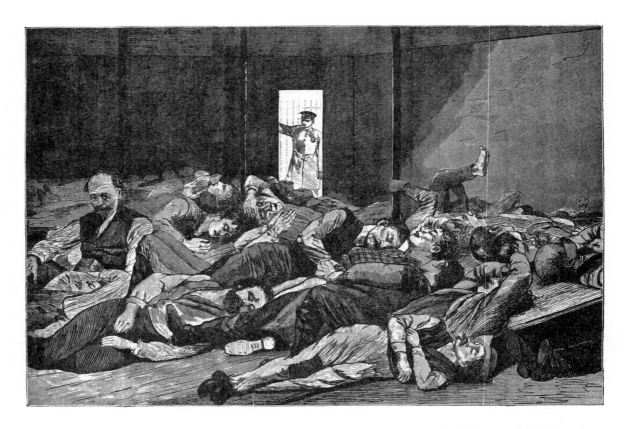

STATION-HOUSE LODGERS, 1874 (Top). Visiting the 17th Precinct station house past midnight in the depths of winter, Winslow Homer drew these 50 homeless men sleeping on the basement floor because they had nowhere else to go. *Harper's* editors reflected on what they called "the shadow of New York"—the desolate conditions in which fully half the city lived in cold, unventilated, overcrowded tenements or, worse, roaming the streets, sleeping in doorways, alleys, on the piers along the waterfront, living in the gutter, prey to hunger, cold, disease, crime, and early death in prison or the almshouse. Throughout the century the city's population of poor was enormous and constantly growing, presenting huge problems with which the city never really dealt. (*Harper's Weekly*; February 7, 1874; Winslow Homer.) UNDERGROUND LODGINGS, 1869 (Bottom). A typical cellar in Greenwich Street, one of the areas where the city's huge vagrant population found lodging on winter nights. A room was filled with 20 or 30 men who were charged 10 to 25 cents for a space in which to sleep. (*Harper's Weekly*; February 20, 1869; P. Frenzeny.)

SQUATTERS, 1869. The majority of New York's poor found refuge in tenement houses and basement rooms in the older parts of the city but throughout the century, a considerable number lived in encampments, such as this one near Central Park, of dilapidated shanties on hilly, broken land for which no commercial or residential use had yet been found. Not until the very end of the century were the last of the squatters, with their goats, geese, chickens and pigs, driven from Manhattan Island, despite their efforts to resist the constant northward development of the city. (*Harper's Weekly*; June 26, 1869; D. E. Wyand.)

ITALIAN BOYS IN NEW YORK, 1873. In the 1870s New Yorkers became aware that young Italian boys were being kidnapped or purchased in Italy and brought to New York to make a living for their masters by begging on the streets. The forlorn children seen here are being taught to perform as a small orchestra with the monkey on the left. *Harper's* and others campaigned vigorously against this practice and in several years were able to report that it was somewhat on the decline. It remained to some degree, however, throughout the century. (*Harper's Weekly;* September 13, 1873; A. Goult and B. Mayrand.)

POOR AT A STEAM GRATING, 1876. A *Harper's* correspondent noticed that on cold winter nights homeless children would gather together at those points in lower Manhattan where warm air was expelled from steam-heated buildings and would spend the night there, taking turns warming themselves at the grates. In this illustra- tion, entitled "The Hearth-Stone of the Poor" a group of poor chil- dren gather at a steam grate on the sidewalk while a prosperous family, of which only the children seem aware of the scene in front of them, passes in the background. (*Harper's Weekly*; February 12, 1876; Sol Eytinge, Jr.)

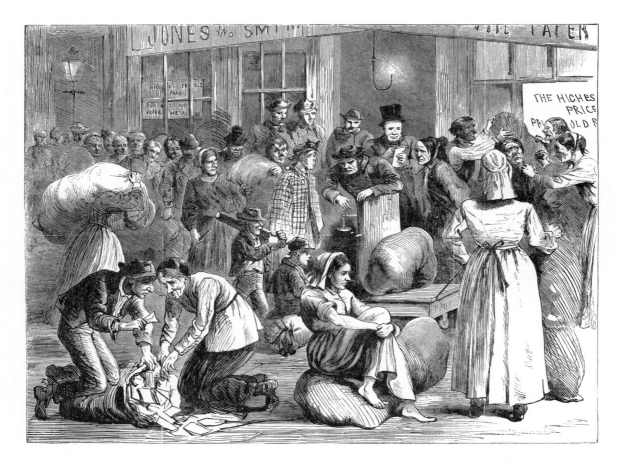

THE BEACH STREET DUMPING BARGE, 1866 (Top). The extreme poverty in which an increasing percentage of New York's population lived as the century wore on may be appreciated from this view, drawn by Stanley Fox, of men, women and children scavenging through garbage on a barge at the foot of Beach Street (now Ericsson Street) on the lower Hudson River waterfront. Anything of any value that might be found—bones, coal, rags, etc., would be saved and sold for pennies. *Harper's* reported, "the meagre pittance obtained in return is spent for a little bread and as much bad whisky as can be bought." (*Harper's Weekly*; September 29, 1866;

Stanley Fox.) RAGPICKERS DISPOSING OF THEIR HAUL, 1868 (Bottom). A group of ragpickers selling their day's haul to an Ann Street dealer. The ragpickers worked early because they had to be done before the city's street-sweepers began at six every morning. Rags might bring two to four cents a pound while a pound of waste paper was worth one to three cents. On a good day a ragpicker earned less than a dollar; disputes frequently arose over territorial rights among the ragpicking population of America's greatest city. (*Harper's Weekly*; November 14, 1868; Paul Frenzeny.)

RAGPICKER, 1870 (Top). This engraving reproduced, in slightly altered form, a London *Graphic* illustration of a New York ragpicker based on a drawing by the English artist Arthur Boyd Houghton. According to *Harper's*, a ragpicker of the time could earn six or seven dollars a week; some had managed to accumulate enough that way to leave the city for a farm in the Western states. (*Harper's Weekly*; May 7, 1870; Arthur Boyd Houghton.) ARRESTED RAGPICKERS, 1867 (Bottom). More than 50 ragpickers were arrested by the police on June 20, 1867 because they hadn't paid their license fees. They were detained for a time in City Hall Park with the dog-carts in which they collected saleable rags from the city's garbage. (*Harper's Weekly*; July 6, 1867; C. G. Bush.)

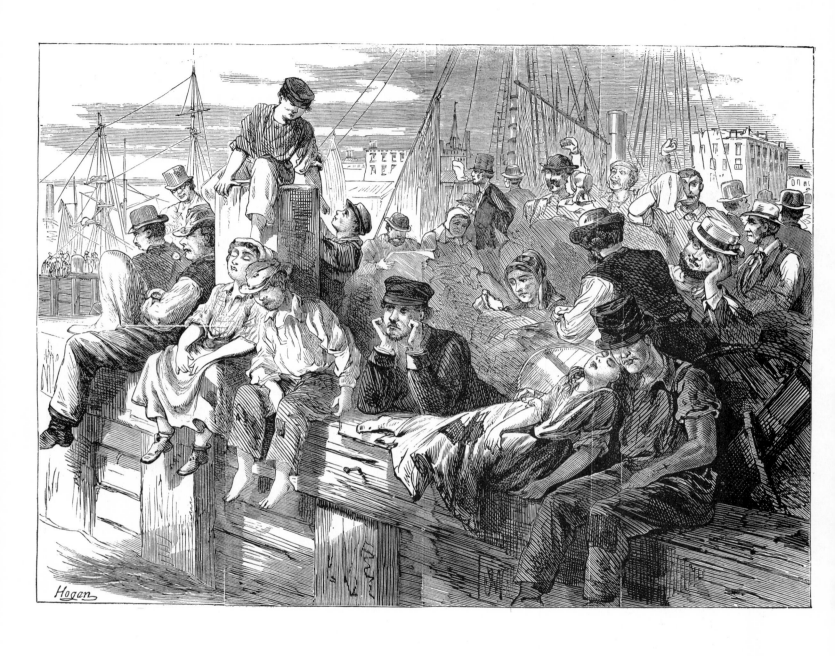

ON THE DOCKS IN THE SUMMER, 1868. Middle-class and wealthy New Yorkers coped with the heat of summer by heading for country and seaside resorts, but the only respite for the poor was on the docks. Even Central Park, *Harper's* claimed, offered limited access to the poor because transportation to it from the city's slums was difficult and expensive—much more difficult than it would be later, during the age of the subway. (*Harper's Weekly*; August 22, 1868; Thomas Hogan.)

TENEMENT LIFE DURING A HEAT WAVE, 1879. A scene just before
daybreak during a hot spell with people sleeping on roofs and in the streets.
(*Harper's Weekly*; August 9, 1879; Sol Eytinge, Jr.)

HEAT WAVE AMONG THE TENEMENTS, 1883 (Above). A night scene on the roof of a lower East Side tenement as men, women and children seek some refuge from the oppressive conditions inside by sleeping, or just sitting if it is too hot to sleep, wherever they can find a little air. (*Harper's Weekly*; June 30, 1883; W. A. Rogers.) RAG-PICKER'S COURT, MULBERRY STREET, 1879 (Opposite). For a series of articles on the tenements of New York, *Harper's* artist William A. Rogers visited this alley known as "Rag-Picker's Court" off Mulberry Street near Chatham Square on the lower East Side. The place was aptly named;

rags, picked off the city's streets and garbage dumps are hanging to be cleaned by sun and rain before being sold for pennies while down below men and women come in with their latest haul. "The men who live in these wretched hovels," *Harper's* reported, "pay from five to six dollars a month rent of earnings that hardly ever exceed fifty cents a day. The agent who lets the property lives in New Jersey. The owner—well, if the name were mentioned, it would surprise the people of New York City." An old story. (*Harper's Weekly*; April 5, 1879; William A. Rogers.)

A Sour-Krer Cellar.

Interior of the Court.

The Home of Five Men.

Children of the Neighborhood.

Entrance of the Alley.

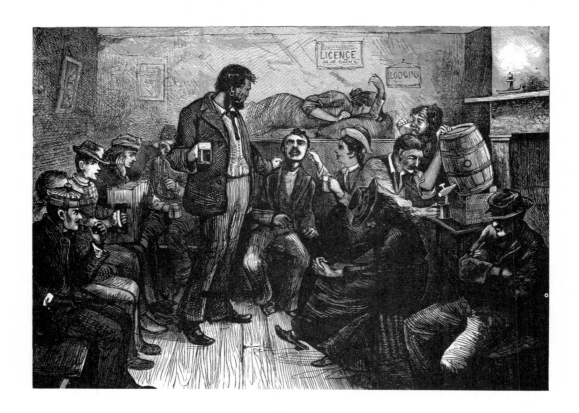

"BOTTLE ALLEY," 1879 (Opposite). Tenement life in 'Bottle Alley' near Chatham Square. (*Harper's Weekly*; March 22, 1879; William A. Rogers.) A "BOTTLE ALLEY" SALOON, 1880 (Top). Artist C. A. Keetels visited this dingy beer saloon in "Bottle Alley" off Baxter Street in the Five Points region in the company of a city policeman. It was in hundreds, perhaps even thousands, of haunts such as this that New York's huge criminal class found refuge from both the police and the reformers who seldom followed them there. (*Harper's Weekly*; February 28, 1880; C. A. Keetels.) SOUP-HOUSE, 1874 (Bottom). As the depression following the Panic of 1873 deepened, New Yorkers responded with intensified charity for the poor and unemployed. In February, 1874, James Gordon Bennett, publisher of the *New York Herald*, donated $30,000 for the maintenance of free soup kitchens throughout the winter in several precincts of the city. Used to doing things in a big way, Bennett engaged the city's premier restaurateur, Lorenzo Delmonico, and his legendary chef, Charles Ranhofer, to supervise the preparation of the soups—a different one each day for variety, each made from the best ingredients obtainable. Theodore R. Davis drew the sketch for this engraving at the Sixth Ward soup kitchen at 110 Centre Street where over 500 people were served on the first day of the program. (*Harper's Weekly*; March 7, 1874; Theodore R. Davis.)

STREET VENDORS, 1877 (Top). A street vendor of fruits and vegetables in a run-down neighborhood. Although they undersold the regular markets, their goods were often spoiled and unhealthy. (*Harper's Weekly*; September 22, 1877; W. M. Cary.) THE HESTER STREET MARKET, 1884 (Bottom). A view of the open-air market established during the 1880s on Hester Street in the predominantly Jewish Polish section of the lower East Side. Clothes, food and all manner of other objects, new and secondhand, were actively sold and traded, a custom which has continued in New York well into the twentieth century. The market was busiest on Friday afternoons and although it was, strictly speaking, against the law, the city's police did not interfere. (*Harper's Weekly*; May 3, 1884; A. Berghaus.) THE SWEATSHOPS, 1890 (Opposite). A view of life on the lower East Side in 1890. The family of an immigrant tailor brings him the garments he is to sew together at the rate of perhaps fifty cents for sixteen hours work. Rogers' drawing is strikingly reminiscent of Jacob Riis' famous photographs of tenement life at the end of the century. (*Harper's Weekly*; April 26, 1890; W. A. Rogers.)

W·A·Rogers.

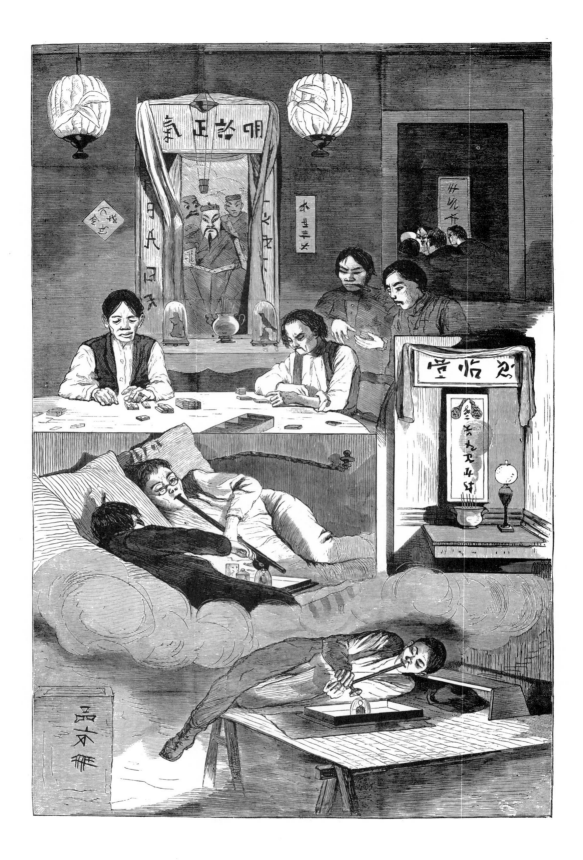

CHINESE CLUBHOUSE, 1874. When Winslow Homer went to sketch a Chinese clubhouse in Baxter Street (just to the west of the present center of New York's Chinatown around Mott and Pell Streets) the Chinese community in the city was still very small—the first Chinaman to settle in New York had arrived only in 1858 and by 1880 the city's Chinese population numbered only about 700. Homer, *Harper's* said, sat for hours with the somewhat malevolent faces of the gods beaming down on him from a wall altar in front of which incense burned and an offering of stuffed birds was placed while in this room and the one seen at the upper right, Chinese sailors gambled with dominoes, playing a single simple game of odd or even. The walls are decorated with scrolls bearing club rules and news of the Celestial Empire. In one place was a small altar, with incense and a lamp burning before a scroll listing the names of dead members; in another room Homer encountered the opium-smokers reclining on low beds and benches as pictured here. The artist reported that he waited in vain to meet the wives of the members of the club, all of whom he was told were Irish or American as there was not then and had not been for some years any Chinese women in New York. Chinese immigration was stopped for a time by the Chinese Exclusion Act of 1882 but New York's Chinatown continued to grow during the last decades of the century, passing through a violent period of gang warfare (the tong wars). By 1910, when peace was finally well established, the community's population was roughly 15,000. (*Harper's Weekly*; March 7, 1874; Winslow Homer.)

SUMMER ON BROADWAY, 1859. The crowded, pushing, congested street scene, full of life, contrasts with the stately portico of St. Paul's Chapel, still standing on the west side of Broadway between Fulton and Vesey Streets. Such a scene, though no doubt here drawn satirically, was probably not too different from what a guest at the Astor House, the great hotel just north of St. Paul's, might have witnessed from his window on a typically busy summer day. Throughout the century, Broadway was the center of New York life. Before midcentury, Broadway below 14th Street was gradually transformed from the city's most fashionable residential area into its leading commercial and shopping district. Later in the century, as the city grew north, lower Broadway retained its commercial character. The stretch from Madison Square to 42nd Street functioned as the center for the city's new hotels and theatrical life. Fifth Avenue became New York's most fashionable residential address, first below and then above 42nd Street. (*Harper's Weekly*, August 27, 1859; Alfred Fredericks.)

THE LOEW BRIDGE, 1867 (Opposite, Top). Broadway, looking south from Ann Street with St. Paul's Chapel (right) and the just-completed *Herald* building (left) on the site of Barnum's first New York museum. Spanning Broadway at Fulton Street, often described as the busiest intersection in the city at this time, is the Loew Bridge, an iron pedestrian crossing which had been built in 1866 at the urging of Philip Genin, a prominent hatter whose building was on the southwest corner. Genin argued that the dense horse-drawn traffic, obvious here, made people reluctant to cross Broadway to visit his shop as well as the others on the west side of Broadway. The bridge was a novelty, but once it wore off another hatter, Knox, on the northeast corner, argued that the structure was unsuccessful and deprived his store of sunlight. Knox won the argument and the Loew Bridge was removed in 1868, a short-lived experiment. The *Herald* building, considered very modern and almost fireproof because of the amount of iron used in its construction, was the home of the paper until it moved in 1893 to the building designed for it by McKim, Mead and White at Herald Square. (*Harper's Weekly*; June 8, 1867; from a photograph by Rockwood.) CROSSING BROADWAY, 1870 (Opposite, Bottom). (*Harper's Weekly*; March 12, 1870; Sol Eytinge, Jr.) THE FARRAGUT FUNERAL, SEPTEMBER 30, 1870 (Above). The funeral of Admiral David Glasgow Farragut, Commander of the Union Fleet during the Civil War, rivaled the Lincoln procession in the size of the crowds. Thousands stood in a driving rainstorm to watch the coffin as it was carried up Broadway and Fifth Avenue to the train which took it to Woodlawn Cemetery for burial. The procession is seen here passing the Metropolitan Hotel on Broadway at Prince Street. Next to it is Niblo's Garden, one of the city's leading theaters of the period. (*Harper's Weekly*; October 15, 1870; Theodore R. Davis.)

DECORATION DAY, 1882. Union Square was 19th-century New York's most popular meeting place for parades and demonstrations of all kinds. Here a solemn crowd of New Yorkers gathers to watch festoons and a wreath being draped around Richard Upjohn's pedestal for H. K. Brown's statue of Washington. (*Harper's Weekly*; June 3, 1882; William St. J. Harper.)

DEMONSTRATION IN UNION SQUARE, 1882. A workingman's demonstration in Union Square on September 5. At that time the issues confronting labor included, as seen from the signs being carried by this well-behaved crowd, the eight-hour day and, above all, the need for more organization, especially at election time. It is interesting to note that the scale of most of the buildings surrounding the Square remains today just about what it was when this view was drawn. (*Frank Leslie's*; September 16, 1882.)

FIFTH AVENUE HOTEL, 1859. (Opposite, Top). The Fifth Avenue Hotel, designed by William Washburn, was built in 1856–58 by financier Amos R. Eno on the west side of Fifth Avenue between 23rd and 24th Streets, where Fifth Avenue and Broadway join at Madison Square. Fifth Avenue was opened in sections during the first half of the nineteenth century. In 1838 the section from 21st Street to 42nd Street was completed, leading to the establishment of Madison Square as a residential area in 1847. It was Eno's intention to build on Madison Square the most magnificent hotel in New York and he succeeded with this six-story white marble building. Accommodating 800 guests, it boasted lavishly decorated public rooms, a fireplace in every bedroom, many private bathrooms (a novelty) and one of the first passenger elevators in the city. Despite some critics who called the hotel "Eno's folly," thinking it was too far uptown to succeed as anything but a summer resort, and others, such as the writer for *Harper's*, who felt the rosewood and silk furnishings too costly for the guests to be comfortable with, the hotel prospered from the start, inaugurating the era when Madison Square became the center of New York's fashionable world. Visiting royalty stayed there, Wall Street financiers took to meeting there after the stock markets closed in the afternoon, and Republican politicians made the hotel their headquarters for plotting strategy during and long after the Civil War. In 1908, when the center of the city's hotel life had moved farther uptown to the neighborhood of the Plaza at 59th Street, the Fifth Avenue Hotel was demolished and its place was taken by an office building. (*Harper's Weekly*; October 1, 1859.) THE DINING ROOM OF THE FIFTH AVENUE HOTEL, 1859 (Opposite, Bottom). When the hotel opened, the basic rate was $2.50 a day, including *four* meals. Guests returned to the second-floor dining room, shown here, to enjoy a late evening supper at the large tables which seated a dozen or more. This was one of the innovations of Col. Paran Stevens, who leased the hotel from Eno. (*Harper's Weekly*; October 1, 1859.) BROADWAY IN WINTER, 1872 (Above). *Harper's* reported that when snow was plowed from the streets, it was piled along the curbs, and that, when mild weather came, the streets turned into rivers of slush. Here a member of the Police Department's Broadway Squad is seen helping an attractive young lady over the slush to a horsecar just outside the Hoffman House, one of the elegant new hotels in the Madison Square area on Broadway near 24th Street, just a bit north of the Fifth Avenue Hotel. (*Harper's Weekly*; March 9, 1872; W. J. Hennessey.)

MADISON SQUARE, 1889. An elegant group out for a Saturday afternoon stroll in Madison Square, the fashionable center of the city. The obelisk of the Worth monument is in the background. (*Harper's Weekly*; November 23, 1889; T. de Thulstrup.)

FIFTH AVENUE, 1859. A panoramic view of New York City looking south along Fifth Avenue from the New Brick Church at 37th Street. One can scan the entire city in vain for a building other than a church that is taller than six or seven stories. In the distance, on the left is Brooklyn; between Brooklyn and Staten Island (which is in the center) is the Narrows, the entrance to the harbor; New Jersey is on the right. The view encompasses most of the developed portion of the city at that time. Many rows of residential brownstones, which would dominate the city's domestic architecture for the rest of the century, are seen here in the relatively recently settled streets in the foreground, including Fifth Avenue itself, at this time a street of brownstone stoops which had been developed over the preceding 20 years. Some larger commercial structures are on the left, toward the old East River waterfront area. The large lawns, empty lots and greenhouse and gazebo farther uptown reveal that New York's development in these areas was far from complete. A suburban feeling still remains here. Brick Presbyterian Church, the spire of which dominates the foreground, was demolished in 1938. (*Harper's Weekly*; April 23, 1859; DeWitt C. Hitchcock, from a photograph by Mathew Brady.)

THE STEWART MANSION, 1869 (Above). Alexander Turney Stewart, one of New York's wealthiest merchants and owner of the fashionable department store at Ninth Street on Broadway, spent three million dollars building his palatial marble home on the northwest corner of Fifth Avenue and 34th Street. When it was completed in 1869, the editors of *Harper's*, in raptures over what they considered a building which surpassed anything yet attempted anywhere in the world, wrote of it "New York is a series of experiments, and every thing which has lived its life and played its part is held to be dead, and is buried, and over it grows a new world . . . But there is one edifice in New York that if not swallowed up by an earthquake, will stand as long as the city remains. . . ." *Harper's* could hardly have been more wrong about the future of the Stewart mansion. The irascible, reclusive Stewart lived there until his death in 1876 and his widow maintained the home until she died ten years later. In 1891 the building was leased by the Manhattan Club but it proved too expensive to maintain and in 1901, only 32 years after it was completed, the Stewart palace was demolished and replaced by the building designed by Stanford White for the Knickerbocker Trust Co. While it stood, however, the Stewart mansion was a symbol for New Yorkers of a new more prosperous and ostentatious age; it ushered in a period when the city's millionaires spent fortunes trying to top each other over and over again with chateaux on Fifth Avenue, each more elaborate and ornate than the last, some of which would make archi-

tect John Kellum's design for Stewart's house seem severe by comparison. (*Harper's Weekly*; August 14, 1869; from a photograph by Rockwood.) THE VANDERBILT MANSIONS, 1885 (Opposite, Top). Among New York's best-known private residences during the last two decades of the century were these twin houses built on the west side of Fifth Avenue between 51st and 52nd Streets for William H. Vanderbilt, son of the Commodore and the richest man in America at that time. He lived in the southernmost house (left) and his two sons-in-law, Elliott F. Shepard and William D. Sloane, jointly occupied the other one with their families. Designed by Charles Atwood and John Snook and completed in 1884, a year before Vanderbilt's death, the motivating factor behind their construction was the family's desire to outdo the A. T. Stewart mansion. With the expenditure of six or seven million dollars, Vanderbilt probably succeeded. Like Stewart's house, the Vanderbilt mansion included an art gallery to which (unlike Stewart's), the public was admitted by invitation one day a week to view the paintings by such popular artists as Turner, Alma-Tadema, Millais, Meissonier and Corot. The Vanderbilt mansions were razed during the 1940s. (*Harper's Weekly*; December 19, 1885; from a photograph by Pach.) THE VANDERBILT ART GALLERY, 1884 (Opposite, Bottom). A view of William H. Vanderbilt's private art gallery when a reception was held there for the press on December 21, 1884. (*Frank Leslie's*; January 5, 1885.)

SELLING HOT CORN ON THE STREETS, 1868 (Top). (*Harper's Weekly*; September 12, 1868.) DR. KENNION'S STREET COFFEE URN, 1880 (Bottom). The distinguished-looking gentleman on the left is Dr. John Kennion of Brooklyn who set out with this specially designed "coffee-urn cart" to convince people to stop drinking alcohol, which he did by offering them coffee, an alternative stimulant, from porcelain cups and a good piece of bread and butter. We are told that Dr. Kennion's missions among the drunks of Brooklyn were well attended, but what permanent effect they had has gone unrecorded. (*Harper's Weekly*; November 20, 1880; W. A. Rogers.)

STREET ARABS, 1872 (Top). A group of urchins follows a primitive horse-drawn street cleaner. (*Harper's Weekly*; August 3, 1872; Paul Frenzeny.) AMUSEMENT IN PRINTING-HOUSE SQUARE, 1868 (Bottom). Throughout the century the area near City Hall Park was one of the busiest in the city; a good place for these ingenious busi-nessmen to find customers. For five cents one could check one's weight on the scales at left, view the heavens with the telescope in the center or test the power of one's lungs with the contraption on the right. (*Harper's Weekly*; July 25, 1868; Stanley Fox.)

STREETS AFTER A SNOWSTORM, 1884. A crowded unidentified city street after a snowstorm in the winter of 1883–84. The elevated tracks above and the horse-drawn traffic below make a vivid con- trast, exemplifying the period of transition into which the city and the country had entered during the last third of the century. (*Harper's Weekly*; January 12, 1884; George Inness, Jr.)

CARTING SNOW FROM THE STREETS, 1867 (Top). (*Harper's Weekly*; February 9, 1867; Stanley Fox.) A GERMAN BAND, 1879 (Bottom). A band of German street musicians, a common feature of New York's street life during this period of heavy German immigration, depicted in an engraving after a painting by J. G. Brown. *Harper's* reported that these brass bands were gradually sup- planting organ grinders as makers of music on the city's streets. The change was considered an improvement because separate bands did not tend to compete with each other on the same street; in earlier days three or four organ grinders would sometimes play on a single block, with cacophonous results. (*Harper's Weekly*; April 26, 1879; J. G. Brown.)

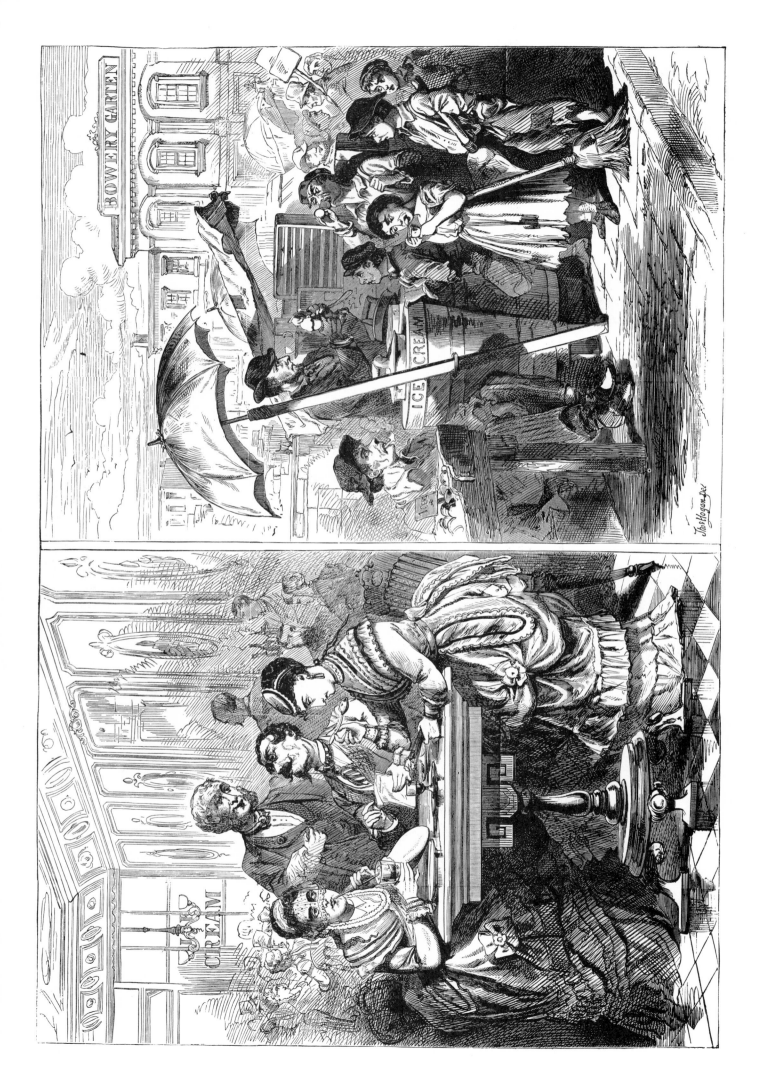

HEAT WAVE, 1868. Another contrast of nineteenth-century life. The temperature is in the nineties and while the fashionable group "on Broadway" on the left takes refuge in an ice cream parlor, the ragged band "in The Bowery" on the right has to find their refreshment from a street vendor. (*Harper's Weekly*, August 15, 1868; Thomas Hogan.)

HEAT WAVE, 1881. A summer "hot wave," as they were then called, provoked *Leslie's* into an illustrated discussion of the common city problem of sunstroke. The tightly corseted woman in this illustration has collapsed on Broadway. The prescribed treatment for sunstroke at this time was rather vigorous: the hospitalized patient was placed on a cot above a large bucket filled with ice; doctors monitored his temperature and pulse while an attendant sprayed ice water over his body. According to *Leslie's*, it seemed to work very well. (*Frank Leslie's*; August 27, 1881; A. B. Shults.)

TWO PICTURE GALLERIES, 1882. The editors of both *Harper's* and *Leslie's* loved to publish pages like this, satirizing the customs of the day while demonstrating the great contrasts of nineteenth-century life. Here we see a crowd at a fashionable upper-class picture gallery and, below, "the people's gallery," a display of advertising art on the brick walls of a New York street. A paradox of changing values: the advertising posters would probably be worth more today than the average painting in this gallery. (*Frank Leslie's*; April 22, 1882.)

SWEEPING BROADWAY AT NIGHT, 1881. A common complaint throughout the second half of the nineteenth century was that the streets of New York were a public disgrace and without question the dirtiest in America. With their Republican sympathies, *Harper's* blamed the generally Democratic city administrations and the patronage system which gave out jobs in the street cleaning department as political favors. Thomas Nast even contributed cartoons to this cause, but the problem remained unsolved. (*Harper's Weekly*, November 12, 1881; H. Muhrman.)

LAYING PAVEMENT, 1869 (Top). New York was a busy city—for example, *Harper's* estimated that in 1869, each day 17,000 vehicles passed the Astor House, Broadway's great and venerable hotel near City Hall. Thus the question of street construction and repair was an important one. Cobblestone streets were no longer laid after 1866; new streets were built and old ones repaired with new paving materials, among them the Fisk concrete method illustrated here. In the Fisk method, a pavement of gravel, broken stone, cinders, coal ash, tar, rosin and asphalt was laid in layers to a total thickness of half to three-quarters of a foot and rolled flat, as is being done in this view. The Fisk concrete was said to have considerable advantages, including increased longevity, over both old and other new paving methods and it was the method adopted by the Commissioners of Central Park for paving the park's carriageways. (*Harper's Weekly*; September 18, 1869; Stanley Fox.) CITY STREET SWEEPERS AT ROLL CALL, 1868 (Bottom). The street sweepers of the period worked from 6 A.M. until 3 or 4 P.M. Here a sleepy-looking band of street sweepers have their roll called by a city inspector before heading out for the day's work. (*Harper's Weekly*; November 14, 1868; Paul Frenzeny.)

JEROME PARK, 1886. In the 1860s New York financier Leonard Jerome, father of Jennie Jerome, Winston Churchill's mother, founded the American Jockey Club with August Belmont and William R. Travers. From its start in 1866, the club's spring and autumn race meetings at Jerome Park in what is now the West Bronx (then part of Westchester County) were highlights of the city's sporting calendar. Members of the Coaching Club drove to the park on fine days and parked their coaches and picnicked, as seen here, on the infield opposite the grandstand, which seated 8000. During the 1880s Jerome Park was the summer equivalent of the Metropolitan Opera—it was the place where fashionable New York came to see and be seen. The park is gone, but Jerome Avenue still preserves the founder's name. (*Harper's Weekly*; June 19, 1886; from a photograph by Bidwell.)

POLO AT JEROME PARK, 1876. A game of polo in progress at the grounds of the Polo Club of New York, not long after the game had been introduced to America by a group of New York sportsmen including James Gordon Bennett, Jr., son of the publisher of the *Herald*. The club had 18 members in the year this view was drawn and attracted large and fashionable crowds to their matches. (*Frank Leslie's*, June 24, 1876, Berghaus & Schimpl.)

A NEW YORK FARO BANK, 1867. It is difficult to estimate the number of gambling houses in New York in the last third of the 19th century; most of the figures we have, coming from anti-gambling sources, seem somewhat inflated. Judging from the literature, however, there were probably a couple of hundred or more, of all types and classes, ranging from the luxurious establishments centered near Broadway in the Madison Square area, catering to the legendary financiers, society figures and politicians, as well as the less opulent houses, such as the one illustrated here, found farther down the side streets. Of all the games played in these houses, faro was undoubtedly the most popular. Artist Francis (Frank) Beard here shows the game as the dealer, seated in the center and the focus of attention, makes "the turn," the moment at which the outcome of the betting is determined. While it is in the nature of the game that any player will lose if he plays long enough, many houses made sure of losses by arranging decks of cards beforehand. The man seated at the right of the table is the "case-keeper," who kept track of the cards that had been played as a reference for gamblers who could calculate their chances. (*Harper's Weekly*; February 23, 1867; Thomas Francis Beard.)

THE DOG SHOW, 1878 (Above). C. S. Reinhart drew this group at the second annual Westminster Kennel Club Dog Show, held at Gilmore's Garden, as the first Madison Square Garden building was known from its opening in 1873 until 1879. The Dog Show, which went on to become a perennial institution in New York life, was immensely popular and well attended even in its first years; *Harper's* reported that almost 1000 dogs (including this mastiff) were exhibited at the 1878 event. (*Harper's Weekly*; May 25, 1878;

drawn by C. S. Reinhart from a sketch by G. H. Stull.) THE HORSE SHOW, 1886 (Opposite). A tandem rig competing at the Madison Square Garden Horse Show in 1886. By this time the show was an annual event of great interest to horse-conscious New Yorkers. In this year 300 first-rate horses were entered. Prizes were awarded for the best in each of several categories: hunters, jumpers, four-in-hand coaches, trotters and small road rigs, among others. (*Harper's Weekly*; November 6, 1886; J. V. Chelminski.)

WOMEN'S DAY AT A PUBLIC BATH, 1872 (Top). Men and women were assigned alternate days at the few free bathing houses which the city had established near the waterfront. The long lines showed that the number of such establishments was grossly inadequate. (*Harper's Weekly*; August 3, 1872; Sol Eytinge, Jr.) A PUBLIC BATH, 1870 (Bottom). A swimming bath for men at the foot of Charles Street on the Hudson River where 200 swimmers, each allowed 30 minutes in the water at a time, could be accommodated. The bath was highly recommended by *Harper's* for all who were unable to leave the city during the heat of August, for in this era these baths provided public hygiene and recreation. (*Harper's Weekly*; August 20, 1870; Stanley Fox.)

LACROSSE, 1883 (Top). New York's first Polo Grounds, just above Central Park at Fifth Avenue and 110th Street, was the setting for the Third Annual Tournament of the U.S. National Lacrosse Association in October, 1883. Six teams, the amateur clubs of New York and Baltimore plus the college teams from Harvard, Yale, Princeton and New York University, competed for the Oelrich Challenge Cup. The Cup had been won by the New York team in 1881 and by Harvard in 1882; at this tournament the New York club regained the title. The winners are seen in this view, which captures the violence of the game, as they defeated Yale in the final game by 2 to 0. (*Harper's Weekly*; November 10, 1883; Taylor & Meeker.)

BASEBALL ON STATEN ISLAND, 1886 (Bottom). The Metropolitan Baseball Club of Staten Island inaugurated its new home field, illustrated here, in the spring of 1886. Located near the ferry landing, a twenty-minute ride from the Battery, the new ballpark attracted large crowds of New Yorkers. The Metropolitans (sometimes, perhaps prophetically, referred to as the "Mets") were a professional club whose league, the American Association, included teams in Brooklyn, Philadelphia, Baltimore, Pittsburgh, Louisville, Cincinnati and St. Louis. When the 1886 Mets were on the road the new field was used for lacrosse games, often featuring highly skilled Canadian teams. (*Harper's Weekly*; May 15, 1886; Schell & Hogan.)

BASEBALL AT THE POLO GROUNDS, 1886. The popularity of baseball was reaching fantastic proportions when this view was drawn of the first National League game of 1886. A crowd of 15,000 paid fifty cents each to watch the New York team go eleven innings to defeat Boston. The National League, most prestigious of the several unrelated "major" leagues then functioning, had been organized in 1876. In 1886 it included teams in New York, Boston, Washington, Philadelphia, St. Louis, Detroit, Chicago and Kansas City. (Harper's Weekly; May 8, 1886; W. P. Snyder.)

COLLEGE FOOTBALL AT THE POLO GROUNDS, 1881. The first game of intercollegiate football had been played between Princeton and Rutgers in 1869; by the 1880s the sport was beginning to take hold. Here an enthusiastic crowd of New Yorkers watches Yale and Princeton in November, 1881. (*Frank Leslie's*; December 17, 1881.)

THE YACHT CLUB REVIEW, 1866 (Above). This large fashionable crowd gathered on the decks of the steam yacht *River Queen* to watch the Second Annual Review of the New York Yacht Club in New York's inner bay on June 19, 1866, as the city returned to normalcy after the Civil War. Those on board must have known that somewhat more than a year earlier, President Lincoln had borrowed the *River Queen* for an abortive peace meeting with Confederate ambassadors. The squadron of racing yachts maneuvering in the background included the fastest yacht then afloat, *Maria*, designed by Robert L. Stevens of Hoboken and a prototype of racing yachts for decades after. The New York Yacht Club, oldest in America, had been founded in 1844 under the leadership of its first Commodore, John C. Stevens. In 1851 he captained the great schooner *America* which defeated England's best and inaugurated a period of American dominance in international yacht racing which has lasted more or less ever since. The annual reviews were grand occasions, marked by elegant dining to the accompaniment of music, and much visiting

from ship to ship throughout the long day on the water. (*Harper's Weekly*; July 7, 1866.) BOAT RACE ON THE HARLEM RIVER, 1875 (Opposite, Top). A boat race between amateur racing clubs on the Harlem River. Spectator boats and contestants for other races crowd the water while in the center we see the two entries in the main event of the day: four-oared boats competing for the grand challenge plate race against each other on the two-mile course from the Fourth Avenue Railroad Bridge to High Bridge. In this race the Athletics Club boat covered the distance in twelve minutes and forty seconds and defeated the Harlem Racing Club crew by more than six lengths. (*Harper's Weekly*; July 17, 1875; J. Davidson.) LIFE-SAVING AT ROCKAWAY, 1877 (Opposite, Bottom). A lifeguard heads out to a swimmer in distress with a life preserver attached to a rope which unwinds from the coil anchored on the beach. The heavy rope extending from the lower left into the water provided bathers with something to hold onto in rough surf. (*Harper's Weekly*; August 25, 1877; C. A. Keetels.)

A WALKING RACE AT GILMORE'S GARDEN, 1879 (Above).
A century ago, when people relied more on walking than they do
today, walking races excited the same sort of interest that basketball
does now. Gilmore's Garden was sold out when an international
walking match was held between the four contestants illustrated
here. O'Leary, third from right, was considered the world champion
at the time, but was out of condition for this race and failed miser-
ably while another man walked off with the first prize. (*Harper's
Weekly*; March 29, 1879; Ivan Pranishnikoff.) THE OLYMPIAN
ROLLER-SKATING RINK, 1885 (Opposite, Top). The rink
opened on Broadway between 52nd and 53rd Streets in January, 1885.
Roller-skating was one of the most popular turn-of-the-century pastimes in the city. (*Frank Leslie's*; January 31, 1885.) A CYCLING
SCHOOL, 1869 (Opposite, Bottom). By the end of the 19th century
cycling was a full-fledged craze in New York. This view of a "Veloci-
pede Riding School" was drawn when the new fad was just gaining a
hold. Velocipedes, the first crank-driven bicycles, were known as
"boneshakers" because of the manner in which they rattled over rough
roads. (*Harper's Weekly*; February 13, 1869.)

CYCLING ON RIVERSIDE DRIVE, 1886 (Above). Cycling, a very popular pastime toward the end of the century, was rigidly controlled. It was not easy to handle these large machines and it was necessary to demonstrate one's proficiency and obtain a badge which served as a permit before the police would allow a rider on the streets. Wheelmen, as the cyclists were called, were allowed to use the full length of Central Park's West Drive from 59th to 110th Streets only between midnight and nine in the morning, and the sport was so popular that the Drive was filled with cyclists during those unlikely hours. The stretch of the Drive between 59th and 72nd Streets, however, could be used at all times, as could Riverside Drive, the favorite road of the wheelmen. Coasting, racing and speeding were strictly prohibited; tricycles had to go single file (bicycles were allowed two abreast); lights were required after sunset and whistles and bells were to be used only in moderation. At the time this view

was drawn the city was said to have 3000 ardent cyclists. (*Harper's Weekly*; July 17, 1886; T. de Thulstrup.) TENNIS IN PROSPECT PARK, 1885 (Opposite, Top). By 1885 the new sport of lawn tennis was making great strides in the New York area. Hundreds of tennis clubs had been formed throughout the city, especially in Brooklyn, where many acres of Prospect Park were being set aside for the game. (*Harper's Weekly*; July 11, 1885; T. de Thulstrup.) AN EX-CURSION STEAMER, 1877 (Opposite, Bottom). On hot summer days tens of thousands of New Yorkers would board side-wheel steamboats for day-long excursions to Coney Island, Rockaway, Long Branch and other resorts in the area. Here is a scene on a bustling East River dock as the crowd boards one of the steamboats with the Manhattan tower of the Brooklyn Bridge in the background. The woman on the left sells bananas and pineapples. (*Harper's Weekly*; September 15, 1877; Charles Kendrick.)

EXCURSION STEAMERS IN ROCKAWAY INLET, 1878. Throughout each summer dozens of these ships were filled with New Yorkers making day-long excursions to Rockaway, Coney Island, Fire Island, and many other resort areas around the city. (*Harper's Weekly*; September 28, 1878; Schell & Hogan.)

FIRE ISLAND, 1873. A chowder party on the beach at Fire Island, already a summer retreat for New Yorkers trying to escape from the heat of the city. (*Harper's Weekly*; August 23, 1873; Thomas Worth.)

AT HIGH BRIDGE, HARLEM RIVER, 1880. A holiday group boards its excursion steamer after enjoying a day amid the rural delights along the banks of the Harlem River. High Bridge, seen at left, conveyed fresh water from Westchester County to the reservoir in Central Park. Note the rowers practicing on the river—one of the most popular sports of the period. The Columbia crew still trains in the area. (*Harper's Weekly*; July 24, 1880; W. A. Rogers.)

THE FOUR-IN-HAND CLUB, 1875. A procession of the Four-In-Hand Club passing through Central Park on the way to the races at Jerome Park in 1875. The imperials on top of the coaches contain picnic lunches, the wicker baskets on the sides were used to hold walking sticks. Servants rode inside the coaches while their employers disported themselves above. (*Frank Leslie's*; November 27, 1875; Albert Berghaus.)

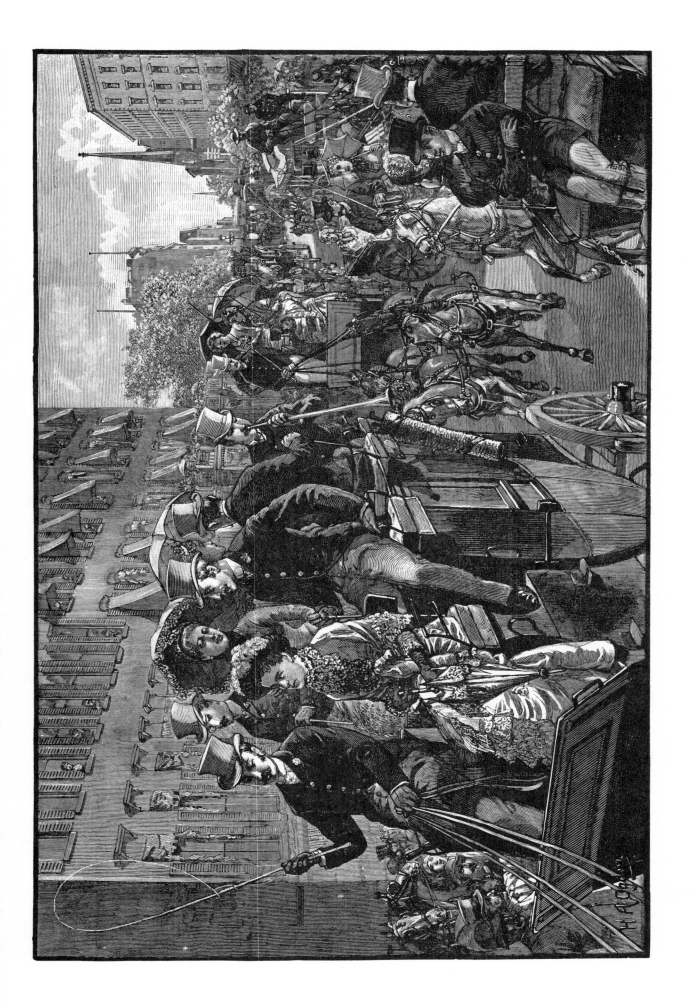

PARADE OF THE NEW YORK COACHING CLUB, 1883. The annual coaching club parade was one of the most picturesque sights New York had to offer in the last century. Millionaires, wearing the club's uniform of brass-buttoned bottle-green coats and white top hats, drove their coaches up a route that usually extended along Fifth Avenue from the Hotel Brunswick at Fifth Avenue and 26th Street to the statue of Daniel Webster in Central Park, near West 72nd Street. The Brunswick (left) was greatly favored by the aristocratic and horsey sets; the Coaching Club was located nearby, at No. 319 Fifth Avenue. The trees of Madison Square can be seen beyond the hotel. On the far right is the Fifth Avenue Hotel. (*Harper's Weekly;* June 2, 1883; H. A. Ogden.)

BALL FOR THE JAPANESE EMBASSY, 1860. During the mid 1850s Admiral Matthew C. Perry led his famous expedition to Japan. In 1860 a group of Japanese ambassadors returned the visit, arriving in New York en route to Washington, and Perry's son-in-law, banker August Belmont, ar- ranged a great ball in their honor on June 18, at the Metropolitan Hotel on Broadway at Prince Street. Five orchestras provided the music to which New Yorkers dined with their Japanese guests at one of the most splendid gatherings ever held by New York society. (*Harper's Weekly*; June 30, 1860.)

CHARITY BALL AT THE METROPOLITAN OPERA HOUSE, 1884. A charity ball held in the Metropolitan Opera House on January 3, 1884—not long after the new building had been opened on October 22, 1883. On these occasions the seats on the orchestra level were boarded over to create a large dance floor level with the stage. (*Frank Leslie's*; January 12, 1884.)

COSTUME BALL AT THE METROPOLITAN OPERA HOUSE, 1890.

(*Frank Leslie's*; February 8, 1890; C. A. Davis.)

HARLEM LANE, 1868. In the years following the Civil War, trotting and trotting horses became a mania with wealthy New Yorkers. The center of trotting activity was the famed Harlem Lane (now St. Nicholas Avenue) between the northern end of Central Park and its junction with the Bloomingdale Road (now Broadway) far out in the country at 168th Street. New Yorkers paused to watch such men as Commodore Vanderbilt, financier August Belmont, actor-manager Lester Wallack, and publisher Robert Bonner drive their rigs up through the residential section of Manhattan and the length of Central Park to reach the Lane. At the northern end the horses, each worth thousands of dollars, were let loose in the fields and were informally raced against each other (with considerable gambling). Stables and inns, such as the one illustrated here, were found at the southern end of the Lane. While activity was greatest on Sunday afternoons, it continued throughout the week. *Harper's* editors may have believed, as they wrote, that "this fleeting procession wears, after all, only the mask of gayety, which hides below it the rottenness and dreary desolation of a life dedicated to fashionable vanities," but the memories of Harlem Lane that have come down to us from those who frequented it leave one with the feeling that this was one of the most unique and enjoyable features of a way of life that long ago vanished from New York. (*Harper's Weekly;* November 21, 1868; Stanley Fox.)

CENTRAL PARK. *The development of Central Park was a unique event in American urban history. When it was begun nothing like it had ever been attempted in America, although it would later be much imitated. Prominent citizens such as William Cullen Bryant and architect Andrew Jackson Downing had long argued the need for a great park available to all New Yorkers and for several years possible sites were debated. There was considerable opinion in favor of Jones' Wood, an area along the East River between 68th and 78th Streets—much smaller than the size of Central Park—but eventually the present site was decided upon. By 1855 the city had acquired, at a cost of $5 million, most of the 843 acres on which Central Park was finally built. At first the proposed park was designed to extend only to 106th Street, but it was later extended to 110th Street. An open competition, judged by Bryant and Washington Irving among others, was held for the design of the new park, and the winner was the plan entitled* Greensward *submitted anonymously by Frederick Law Olmsted and his partner, Calvert Vaux. In 1857 Olmsted was named superintendent in charge of the construction of the park and work began. Olmsted and Vaux' plan was detailed and complex. It called for turning hundreds of acres of dismal, swampy land inhabited by thousands of squatters living in shanties into a fully integrated area of lawns, lakes, footpaths, drives and woods with rocky outcroppings at appropriate places and, one of the designers' best ideas, transverse roads sunk beneath ground level to make them less conspicuous. This huge area devoted to nature in the middle of Manhattan was a completely artificial creation; five million cubic yards of earth and rock were rearranged, over 100 miles of drainage pipe were installed, artificial lakes were dug, trees and brush were carefully planted and landscaped. Although the park was in use virtually from* the time construction began, almost two decades passed before the finishing touches were complete. Olmsted and Vaux fought bitterly in later years with city politicians who handed out patronage jobs in the park to people who were unable to run it; the designers had good reason to charge, as they did, that park authorities sometimes neglected both the basic design of the park and its maintenance. In subsequent decades, despite the politics and the debates between those who would maintain the park's original design and those who would turn sections of it over to purposes undreamt of by Olmsted and Vaux, the park seems to have survived both as a place for recreation for the city's millions and as a work of art in itself. After working on the park Olmsted led an amazingly prolific career of landscape designing (Brooklyn's Prospect Park, Manhattan's Riverside Park, the Boston park system, the campus of Stanford University and the Columbian Exposition in Chicago were only a few of his major projects), but the success of his first great commission, Manhattan's Central Park, has served to link his name inextricably with the life and history of New York City in the nineteenth century.*

A DRIVE IN CENTRAL PARK, 1860. Winslow Homer made the drawing for this engraving of fashionable New Yorkers turned out in their carriages. Despite some complaints about the management of the park's construction, which, *Harper's* asserted, came primarily from disappointed job seekers, the general feeling in the city was that the park was turning out well and would be one of the notable things which could be shown to the Prince of Wales on his impending visit. The trees seen here are just beginning to grow in. (*Harper's Weekly;* September 15, 1860; Winslow Homer.)

CENTRAL PARK: MUSIC ON THE MALL, 1869. A fashionable gathering turned out on a Saturday afternoon in the fall for a concert on Central Park's lushly overgrown Mall. Obviously the music being played in the background is a secondary consideration to socializing. (*Harper's Weekly*, October 9, 1869.)

A CENTRAL PARK DRIVE, 1883. A scene on one of the drives in Central Park on a typical spring day at four o'clock in the afternoon. The city's leading businessmen, their working day over, headed for the Park in appropriate attire at the reins of their custom-built trotting rigs accompanied by groups of friends and relatives, preferably including some good-looking young women. As friends and acquaintances passed each other, they doffed their hats or raised their whips in a salute. (*Harper's Weekly*, May 19, 1883; Gray & Parker.)

HIPPOPOTAMUSES IN THE CENTRAL PARK ZOO, 1888. In the 1880s the Central Park authorities paid $5000 each for these two hippopotamuses which were housed in a tank north of the old Arsenal building near 65th Street on the east side of the park. Great crowds gathered during the summer (in winter, the animals were sent to a warmer climate) to watch the huge African beasts disport themselves, especially during feeding time. Each of them disposed of 600 pounds of grass and 40 pounds of bread each day. (*Harper's Weekly*; September 29, 1888; F. S. Church.)

CENTRAL PARK: THE NORTH MEADOWS, 1889. The North Meadows of Central Park, a 19-acre area just above the 97th Street transverse road, as seen in the fall, when it was used for lawn tennis, croquet, and school picnics. In the winter, people went to the North Meadows to practice walking on their snowshoes. (*Harper's Weekly*; October 5, 1889; W. T. Smedley.)

SKATING IN CENTRAL PARK, 1872. By 1872 the park was
almost finished, some of the trees had grown tall and in the winter
ice skating was the greatest fad. Men, women and children flocked to
the park by the thousands to spend their free time on the ice. In the

background is Bow Bridge. The total absence of a city skyline intruding on the park makes it really seem like being in the country. (*Harper's Weekly*; February 17, 1872; Jules Tavernier.)

SKATING IN CENTRAL PARK, 1877. An elegant skating party on one of the Central Park lakes. (*Harper's Weekly;* February 24, 1877; Schell & Hogan.)

SLEIGHING IN CENTRAL PARK, 1886. A mounted policeman watching a fashionable parade of horse-drawn sleighs on Central Park's West Drive in 1886. Policemen on park duty were provided with horses fast enough to catch runaways and speeders, although this crowd seems to have their horses well in hand. The sleighs are seen here passing Thomas Ball's bronze statue of Daniel Webster which had been erected in 1876. (Webster's Napoleonic pose is accurately drawn here, but artist W. P. Snyder's hastily drawn face is nothing like Ball's conception of Webster). Architect Henry J. Hardenbergh's Dakota apartments, in the background at 72nd Street and Central Park West, had been completed only two years before this view was drawn and still overlooks this scene. (Harper's Weekly; February 27, 1886; W. P. Snyder.)

SLEIGHING IN CENTRAL PARK, 1890. The winter of 1889–90 was unusually mild, but a brief period of heavy snow at the beginning of March brought out all the sleighs which had lain idle. *Harper's* reported that it cost at least twice as much to rent a sleigh than a carriage; during a typical New York winter there were so few days on which sleighs could be used that those in the sleigh rental business had to make all they could while they could. (*Harper's Weekly*; March 15, 1890; T. de Thulstrup.)

RIVERSIDE PARK, 1880. In 1868 work started on the first section of Riverside Park, along the Hudson River on Manhattan's then scarcely-settled upper West Side; a few years later the project was turned over to Olmsted and was almost finished when *Harper's* published this view. The long narrow park, with its drive beside the water, has come to be considered one of the prolific Olmsted's greatest accomplishments. (*Harper's Weekly*; April 24, 1880; Granville Perkins from a sketch by A. L. Jackson.)

THE CONEY ISLAND CONCOURSE, 1877 (Above). A pivotal year, 1877 saw the opening of the Coney Island Concourse, a mile and a half of paved concrete road 250 feet wide, running parallel to the surf. The road was an extension of the lower end of King's Highway which connected Coney Island to Brooklyn. With this new broad avenue for carriages and the handsome pavilions on the beach illustrated here, along with many other novelties and attractions, *Harper's* accurately predicted that the next years would see a vast increase in Coney Island's already great popularity. With its beaches, hotels and amusement parks within easy reach by rail or boat, Coney Island became the dominant New York summer resort during the second half of the century, undergoing many great changes in the process. (*Harper's Weekly*; August 4, 1877; Schell &

Hogan.) THE BRIGHTON BEACH FAIR GROUNDS, 1879 (Opposite, Top). One of the great attractions of Brighton Beach in the late 1870s was this new racecourse, the Brighton Beach Fair Grounds. Located near the Brighton Beach Hotel and railroad station, it boasted a well-constructed track a mile long, an additional steeplechase course, stables for 200 horses, a hotel just for jockeys and trainers, and two grandstands (seats in the one closer to the finish line were more expensive). (*Harper's Weekly*; August 30, 1879; Paul Frenzeny.) CLAMMING AT CONEY ISLAND, 1884 (Opposite, Bottom). Crowds of New Yorkers are seen here digging for clams on the beaches of Coney Island. The inset picture shows crow-hunting along Coney Island Creek. (*Harper's Weekly*; March 8, 1884; Albert Berghaus.)

CROWS ALONG CONEY ISLAND CREEK.

CONEY ISLAND, 1883. *Harper's* artist Charles Graham climbed to the top of an observatory at Coney Island to sketch this view looking east along the beach with its row of fashionable hotels. While the resort was considered unparalleled as a place for summer recreation, *Harper's* claimed at the time this view was published that some parts of Coney Island had been virtually taken over by gamblers whose presence was becoming increasingly oppressive to the majority of the travelers who visited there. The absence of the huge crowds which are such a common feature of photographs of Coney Island made just a few years after this view was drawn indicates that the era of its greatest popularity was yet to come. (*Harper's Weekly*; August 11, 1883; Charles Graham.)

FIREWORKS AT MANHATTAN BEACH, 1885. Among the things for which Coney Island became justly famous toward the end of the nineteenth century were the magnificent fireworks displays which lit up the skies for miles on summer evenings. This elaborate display was an historical tableau, with live actors, depicting scenes from *The Last Days of Pompeii*, complete with an artificial lake in front of a huge stage setting. Accompanied by appropriate music, the presentation was climaxed by fireworks representing the destruction of the city by the eruption of Mt. Vesuvius. (*Harper's Weekly*; July 25, 1885; Charles Graham.)

A CONEY ISLAND ROLLER COASTER, 1886. It cost a nickel to make the complete one-minute trip on this primitive roller coaster which had been erected two years earlier and was from the start a great success (*Frank Leslie's*; July 24, 1886.)

UNDER THE HOTEL

MOVING THE BRIGHTON BEACH HOTEL, 1888. In the winter of 1887–88 it became clear that rough seas were undermining Coney Island's Brighton Beach Hotel. Railroad tracks were laid up to the hotel and on April 3, 1888, the locomotives began moving it 600 feet inland. The hotel opened for business as usual that summer. *Leslie's* published this engraving in anticipation of the event; actually only six locomotives were used, in three teams of two each. (*Frank Leslie's*; January 14, 1888.)

LIFESAVING AT CONEY ISLAND, 1889. (*Frank Leslie's*; August 24, 1889; J. Durkin.)

FRANCONI'S HIPPODROME, 1853 (Top). Franconi's Hippodrome, built in 1853 for $200,000, stood on the west side of Broadway opposite Madison Square between 23rd and 24th Streets. The two-story brick outer wall, covered by a canvas roof 80 feet high, enclosed an oval one-sixth of a mile around. Ten thousand spectators could be accommodated for displays of horsemanship, gymnastics and such novel entertainments as the opening-night chariot races. New Yorkers turned out enthusiastically at first, but the Hippodrome's success was short-lived. Abandoned within two years, the site was appropriated for the new and fashionable Fifth Avenue Hotel which opened in 1859. (*Illustrated News*; March 19, 1853.)

BARNUM'S AMERICAN MUSEUM, 1853 (Bottom). P. T. Barnum established his American Museum at Broadway and Ann Street late in 1841 by purchasing, from the estate of its founder, Scudder's Museum, which had occupied the building since 1830. He enlarged the structure in 1843 and in 1850, constantly adding to the collec-

tions and in a few years he had turned it into a flourishing center of popular entertainment. The fare he offered his credulous public was nothing if not varied—a large menagerie, coins, works of art, wax figures, the Swiss bearded lady, the "wooly-headed Albino woman," and the first Siamese twins to be displayed in America. His star attractions were the famous midgets, General Tom Thumb (Charles S. Stratton) and his bride Lavinia Warren Bumpus. The large, well-appointed lecture room–theater was often the venue for melodrama with a temperance theme, a favorite cause of the founder; in 1850 *The Drunkard* became the first New York play to achieve an uninterrupted 100-performance run. The American Museum was destroyed in a spectacular fire on July 13, 1865, one of the many fires that seemed to haunt Barnum's life. He lost two other New York museums to fire in 1868 and 1872; in 1857 his fantastic Oriental-style estate, *Iranistan*, burned to the ground in Bridgeport. (*Illustrated News*; October 29, 1853.)

THE TRANSFER OF JUMBO FROM THE BATTERY TO MADISON SQUARE GARDEN, 1882. Nothing that P. T. Barnum had done since sponsoring the American tour of Jenny Lind in the early 1850s matched the excitement caused in New York by the arrival of Jumbo, the largest elephant ever exhibited. Barnum had purchased the six-and-a-half-ton animal, which stood eleven and a half feet high, for $10,000 from London's Royal Zoological Gardens. The beast was immensely popular in England and the sale had been protested in the papers, in the courts and in Parliament. The sale went through, however, and Barnum's great prize arrived in New York on board the *Assyrian Monarch* on Easter Sunday, 1882, to be greeted by huge cheering crowds. Sixteen horses were not sufficient to pull Jumbo and a couple of Barnum's smaller elephants, as illustrated here, had to push the specially-constructed truck from behind as the procession made its way from the Battery to Barnum's circus headquarters at Madison Square Garden, where the great showman's activities were centered late in the century. Once installed, Jumbo had a brief but spectacular career. New Yorkers and tourists flocked to the circus to see the new attraction; books and articles chronicled every facet of his life including his well-publicized walk across the Brooklyn Bridge and his prodigious appetite which favored whiskey, beer, candy and sweet rolls. Jumbo was killed by a railroad train in St. Thomas, Ontario, in September, 1885, barely three and a half years after his American debut. His skeleton is on display at the American Museum of Natural History in New York while his stuffed skin, subsequently destroyed in a fire, was placed with the Natural History Museum of Tufts University. (*Frank Leslie's*; April 22, 1882.)

MADISON SQUARE GARDEN, 1890. *Harper's* published this view of Stanford White's new Madison Square Garden, looking northeast from the Square toward the corner of Madison Avenue and 26th Street, when the building, perhaps the greatest landmark of the 1890s, was still under construction on the block surrounded by Madison and Fourth Avenues and 26th and 27th Streets. It is a good likeness of the finished yellow-brick and terra-cotta building, differing mainly in the pose of the statue on the top of the tower (it does not resemble the elongated figure of Augustus Saint-Gaudens' *Diana* which was eventually installed there) and in the positioning of the windows on the south side of the tower—they were finally placed in regular rows of two each unlike the diamond pattern seen on the west side.

Directly across 26th Street is the University Club, now demolished, which was originally the house of Leonard Jerome, Winston Churchill's grandfather. The larger view shows how the main arena would look. The completed building also included a restaurant, concert hall and the roof garden in which architect White was murdered in 1906. Madison Square Garden was demolished in 1925, after having held innumerable prizefights, other sporting contests, shows and exhibitions of all kinds. It was replaced by the New York Life Insurance Company building. The subsequent Madison Square Gardens were built at Eighth Avenue and 49th Street and above Penn Station at Seventh Avenue and 34th Street. (*Harper's Weekly*, April 12, 1890; Hawley & Snyder.)

MADISON SQUARE GARDEN COLONNADE, 1891. An elegant 1890s crowd under the arcade of Madison Square Garden at night. To contemporaries, the street-level arcades, a feature seldom found in New York's architecture, was one of the most attractive aspects of the building. (*Harper's Weekly*; July 18, 1891; W. T. Smedley.)

JOHN ALLEN'S DANCE HOUSE, 1868. A view of the lively interior of John Allen's Dance House at 304 Water Street where, in the 1850s and 1860s the activities of Allen's girls and their customers earned the proprietor the title of "the wickedest man in New York." Allen was a perplexing character. He considered himself a religious man, and demonstrated his piety by occasionally reading sermons to his staff and making sure that the small rooms set aside for prostitution in the back of his establishment were equipped with Bibles at all times. In 1868 his religiosity backfired when, under the pretext of mending his ways, Allen rented his Dance House for a substantial sum to a group of clergymen who used it to hold prayer meetings. Word got out that Allen's "conversion" had been purchased and when he tried to reopen the old Dance House after the ministers' lease had expired, he found his old regular crowd had abandoned him. Soon Allen was out of business for good. (*Frank Leslie's*, August 8, 1868.)

A BOWERY "MUSEUM," 1881. In the last quarter of the century The Bowery at night presented a scene that was characteristically and uniquely New York. A highly animated world of fruit stands and patent medicine displays, theaters large and small, bars, restaurants of many nationalities (though the German element predominated), and, as illustrated here, various "museums" where for a few cents the credulous could view such curiosities as the fat woman, dwarfs, trained monkeys and other sideshow attractions. (*Harper's Weekly;* February 26, 1881; Henry Muhrman.)

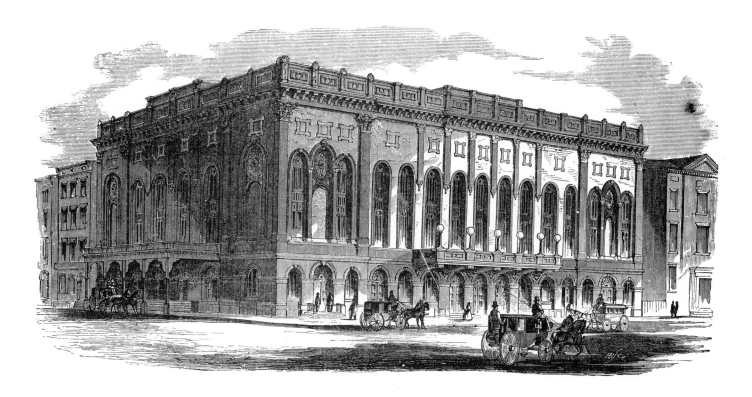

THE ACADEMY OF MUSIC, 1856. Built in 1853–54 on the northeast corner of 14th Street and Irving Place, the Academy of Music was the first opera house to succeed in New York. As opera became increasingly fashionable during the second half of the century, the Academy came to play a crucial role in New York's musical and social life. It was the scene of many receptions and balls, such as that given for the Prince of Wales in 1860. Under the direction of such producers as Max Maretzek and Maurice Strakosch, opera in New York quickly became a tradition. While the 4000 seats of the Academy were occupied by an audience from many levels of society, the upper strata competed for the few boxes. Ultimately an association of wealthy New Yorkers unable to get boxes at the Academy backed the establishment of the new Metropolitan Opera which opened in its new house at Broadway and 39th Street in 1883. The new Met quickly surpassed the Academy. By 1885 the Academy had closed as an opera house, and was eventually replaced by The Consolidated Edison building. (*Ballou's Pictorial Drawing-room Companion*; March 29, 1856.)

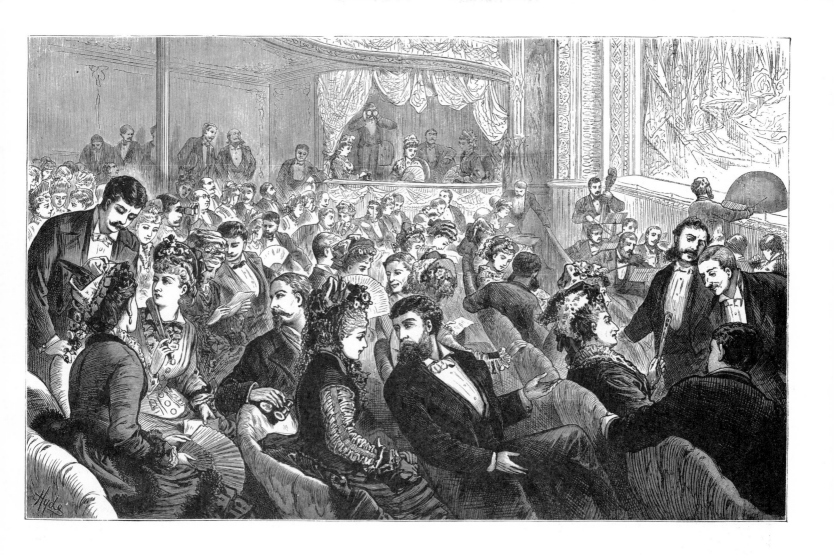

PIKE'S OPERA HOUSE, 1868 (Opposite, Top). *Harper's* considered financier Samuel N. Pike's white-marble and iron Opera House the height of elegance when it opened in 1868 on the northwest corner of Eighth Avenue and 23rd Street. With 2600 seats, 33 boxes and a huge stage, Pike hoped his new building would supplant the Academy of Music as the musical center of the city but, not being in a fashionable neighborhood, it failed to do so. The theater was sold the following year to Jim Fisk and Jay Gould—Fisk had a publicized fondness for the French actresses who performed Offenbach there. They renamed it the Grand Opera House and used the top floors for their Erie Railroad offices while continuing to present light opera in the theater. It was there that Fisk's body lay in state following his murder early in 1872 in a dispute over the affections of his mistress. The Grand Opera House had a long and rich history after Fisk's death. For years Broadway productions featuring leading actors and actresses such as Joseph Jefferson and Lillie Langtree were performed there, and after 1910 George M. Cohan produced plays there. It became a film and vaudeville theater in 1917; vaudeville was discontinued in 1936, but the Grand Opera House survived as a movie theater until it was demolished by fire in 1960. (*Harper's Weekly*; January 25, 1868; from a photograph by Rockwood.) BOOTH'S THEATRE, 1869 (Opposite, Bottom). In 1864–65 New York's most celebrated actor, Edwin Booth, achieved the unprecedented feat of playing Hamlet in New York for 100 consecutive performances, an accomplishment unique in the annals of the city's stage up to that time. At the end of the run a group of prominent New Yorkers appeared on stage and presented Booth with a com-

memorative gold medal. Forced almost immediately afterward into a self-imposed retirement when his brother John Wilkes assassinated Lincoln, Booth was compelled by financial obligations to return to acting and was enthusiastically received by New York audiences who did not bear him malice for the crime of his brother. By 1868 Booth's fortunes had recovered to the extent that his magnificent new theater was ready to open on the southeast corner of Sixth Avenue and 23rd Street. Designed by Renwick and Sands, this elaborate structure of New Hampshire granite was the best equipped theater in the city. Scenery could be raised from below stage level or allowed to sink before the eyes of the audience; a novel ventilation system incorporating a huge fan cooled the theater in summer and warmed it in winter. In case of fire the building could be emptied in minutes. An aesthetic and technological success, Booth's Theatre did not fare as well financially. Built at a cost of over a million dollars raised by a mortgage on Booth's presumed future earnings, the beautiful new theater was undermined by inflation and mismanagement and was dealt a mortal blow by the financial panic of 1873. Five years after the opening, Booth himself was bankrupt. In 1883 the theater was converted into the department store of James T. McCreery and Company. (*Harper's Weekly*; January 9, 1869; from a photograph by Rockwood.) THE LYCEUM THEATRE, 1875 (Above). A fashionable New York theater audience, drawn at the Lyceum Theatre on Fourteenth Street near Sixth Avenue. During the season of 1875–76 the house was devoted to the production of French drama and light opera. (*Frank Leslie's*; December 25, 1875; J. N. Hyde.)

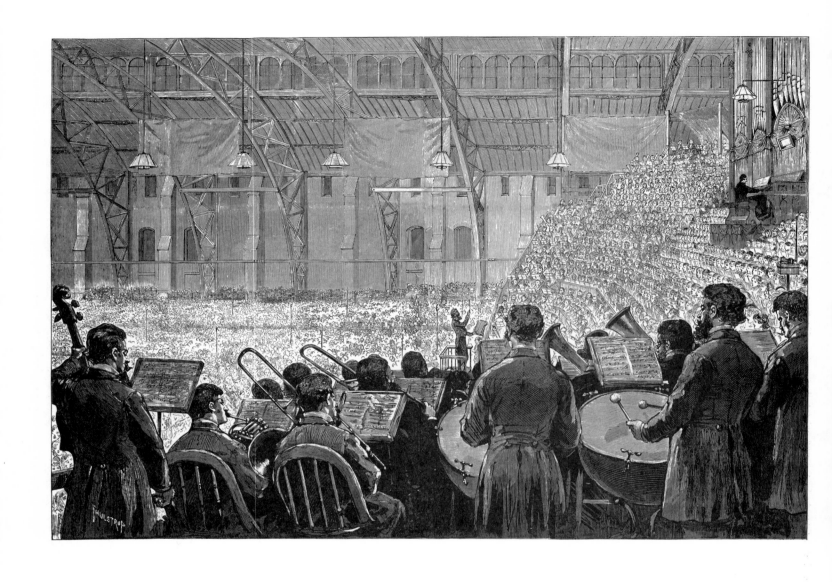

THE MUSIC FESTIVAL IN THE SEVENTH REGIMENT ARMORY, 1881. The cavernous interior of the new Seventh Regiment Armory on Park Avenue between 66th and 67th Streets was the setting for an immense musical festival in May, 1881. Before audiences of 10,000 for each concert, Leopold Damrosch conducted an orchestra of 250 and a chorus of 1200 in performances of the Berlioz Requiem (for which the orchestra was supplemented with four brass bands), Handel's *Messiah*, Rubenstein's *Tower of Babel* and Beethoven's Ninth Symphony. The nucleus of the musicians came from the New York Symphony Orchestra and the Oratorio Society, both of which were normally conducted by Damrosch. The festival was considered a great success, despite the relatively poor acoustics, which were not helped by the way parts of the chorus and orchestra were placed high above the audience. (*Harper's Weekly*; May 21, 1881; T. de Thulstrup.)

SIEGFRIED AT THE METROPOLITAN OPERA, 1887. Italian opera lost so much money during its first seasons at the Metropolitan Opera that the directors soon turned to the German repertory, especially Wagner; German opera was cheaper to produce. *Siegfried* was given its American premiere at the Met on November 9 with Max Alvary (seen here in the second act, doing in the dragon Fafner) as the hero and the incomparable Lilli Lehmann as Brünnhilde. Of the performance, *New York Tribune* critic Henry Krehbiel wrote, "A dragon sings, vomits forth steam from his cavernous jaws, fights and dies with a kindly and prophetic warning to his slayer . . . Finally, an American opera audience was last night compelled to sit during the representation in darkness so dense [a tradition which continues today] that neither shapely shoulders, gorgeous gowns nor dazzling diamonds could delight the eye. . . ." (*Harper's Weekly*; December 3, 1887; Barnard & Graham.)

AFTER THE OPERA, 1890 (Above). A scene at the Metropolitan. The evening's performance over, the fashionable crowd slowly leaves, far more interested, *Harper's* could not resist commenting, in the social parade than in the singing they have just heard. The manners of the wealthy box holders frequently came under attack by music lovers. Visiting between boxes continued throughout the performance, and conversation rarely stopped. (*Harper's Weekly*; March 15, 1890; A. E. Sterner.) THE NATIONAL ACADEMY OF DESIGN, 1865 (Opposite, Top). The white-and-dark-marble Venetian Gothic palace designed by P. B. Wright for the National Academy of Design on the northwest corner of Fourth Avenue and 23rd Street opened in the spring of 1865. The National Academy of Design had been founded in New York in 1826 by a group of American artists led by Samuel F. B. Morse, who also served as its first president. Intended to further the cause of American art by providing both facilities for the instruction of younger artists and for the exhibition of works by established hands, the National Academy was in its early days a rival of the older American Academy of Fine Arts.

National Academy members criticized the older institution as being too exclusive and intellectually and artistically old fashioned— exactly the same charges that a newer generation of young artists would bring against the National Academy itself by the end of the century. The building was demolished in 1901. (*Frank Leslie's*; June 3, 1865.) VARNISHING DAY AT THE NATIONAL ACADEMY, 1870 (Opposite, Bottom). 1870 saw the 45th annual spring exhibition of the National Academy of Design at the still new and controversial building—some artists claimed it had cost more than the Academy could afford. C. S. Reinhart made the drawing for this engraving of Varnishing Day at the National Academy—the last day for artists whose works had been accepted and hung to touch up and varnish the paintings before the rooms were opened to the public. This was serious business for the artists whose careers depended on reputations being made at exhibitions such as this; their task was not made easier by the 19th-century custom of filling the walls completely with pictures so that very few could be shown to their best advantage. (*Harper's Weekly*; May 7, 1870; C. S. Reinhart.)

THE LOAN EXHIBITION AT THE NATIONAL ACADEMY, 1878. For their 1878 loan exhibition, ladies of the Society of Decorative Art borrowed porcelain, silver, lace, embroidery, paintings, clocks, musical instruments, medieval weapons, jewelry and other miscellaneous *objets d'art* from the homes and collections of upper-class New Yorkers. The result was, as in-tended, a panorama of the taste and style which characterized the age. A few decades earlier it would have been more difficult to assemble such a collection in New York. By this date, however, the rooms of the National Academy were easily filled to overflowing. (*Harper's Weekly*, November 2, 1878; from photographs by Pach.)

THE TILE CLUB, 1880. The Tile Club was an informal group of New York artists who, beginning in 1867, met once a week at the studio of one of the members to paint small pictures on Spanish tiles; each week's host receiving as a present the tiles painted at the meeting he sponsored. The club later switched to painting on larger ceramic plaques. As the club evolved, musician friends joined in to provide background entertainment. In the summers, the members of the Tile Club went on expeditions to Long Island and up the Hudson by boat, producing landscapes along the way, many of which were ultimately published in various Harper & Brothers publications and elsewhere. When C. S. Reinhart, himself a member of the Tile Club and a regular *Harper's* illustrator, sketched this view of a meeting in progress, the club included among its members Julian Alden Weir, Harry Chase, R. S. Gifford, Frederick Dielman and other New York artists of the period. (*Harper's Weekly;* January 31, 1880; C. S. Reinhart.)

THE METROPOLITAN MUSEUM, 1889 (Left). A fall reception inaugurated the season at the Metropolitan Museum of Art in 1889, less than a decade after the completion of the museum's first building on Central Park near East 82nd Street. The original building is no longer visible, the Museum having grown around it. This view is of the gallery of Old Masters, which even at this early date housed some of the masterpieces which have been mainstays of the collection ever since—the large painting in the center of the far wall is Van Dyck's portrait of James Stuart, Duke of Richmond and Lennox, which the museum had acquired in 1886. Other artists whose work was seen at this reception included Velasquez, Gainsborough, Turner, Reynolds, Hals and Rembrandt. (*Harper's Weekly*; November 16, 1889; W. T. Smedley.) COPYING AT THE METROPOLITAN MUSEUM, 1888 (Right). An art student paints a copy of Rosa Bonheur's popular *Horse Fair.* Copyists were allowed in the museum on Mondays and Tuesdays but, to prevent fraudulent sales, were forbidden by the directors from making their copies the same size as the originals. (*Frank Leslie's*; May 26, 1888.)

THE CENTURY CLUB, 1889. The elegant Italian Renaissance-style Century Club at 7 West 43rd Street, designed by Stanford White at 26, was completed in 1889–91. Founded by William Cullen Bryant in 1847, the club was one of the most prestigious in New York; many members were connected with the arts or the intellectual life of the city. The original membership of 100 (hence the club's name) has long been exceeded, but the building still stands although its appearance has been altered slightly from the way it looks in this engraving—the open loggia above the doorway is now glassed in, and the finials along the balustrade on the roof are not to be seen. (*Harper's Weekly*; November 2, 1889.)

VOTING IN NEW YORK, 1858. The rougher side of New York City politics in the period just before the Civil War may be seen in this engraving of a saloon at No. 488 Pearl Street as it was used for a voting-place on election day. It is not difficult to imagine some undue influence being exerted here in favor of the "regular Democratic" Irish candidates, whose placards decorate the walls, as voters force their way through to the back room where the ballot boxes are kept. (*Harper's Weekly*; November 13, 1858.)

TAMMANY HALL ON ELECTION NIGHT, 1859. *Harper's* artist J. McNevin went to Tammany Hall on Frankfort Street to sketch this tumultuous scene on election night, November 8, 1859. He found the Tammany crowd particularly intense as it interrupted the reading of the returns from the city's precincts with alternating singing and fighting, for Democratic candidate Fernando Wood was winning his third election to the New York mayoralty and was doing it without official Tammany support. Wood had been unable to maintain control of Tammany following his second term in office which had ended two years before. Wood supporters and regular Tammany Democrats clashed vociferously and physically throughout the night as Wood's majority gradually piled up. (*Harper's Weekly;* November 19, 1859; J. McNevin.)

PROCESSION OF THE WIDE-AWAKES, 1860. A Republican procession carrying the banner of Abraham Lincoln in Printing-House Square on October 3, 1860. The Republicans had borrowed the symbol and slogan ("Wide-Awake") from one of the nativist political parties of the day, the Order of the American Star. In the center is the first *New York Times* building, completed in 1857, replaced on the same site by the second *Times* building in the late 1880s. (*Harper's Weekly*; October 13, 1860.)

TWEED'S COUNTY COURTHOUSE, 1871. The County Court-house (now known as the Municipal Court Building) was completed in 1871 on the western side of City Hall Park. The cupola of City Hall rises on the right. The courthouse was one of the most memorable buildings constructed in New York during the 19th century, not because of its architecture, which is routine, but because of its association with William Marcy Tweed and his "Ring," whose systematic graft, carried to new lengths in the completion of this structure, made it the costliest public building in the United States up to that time—even exceeding the amount spent on the Capitol in Washington, D.C. In 1858 the legislature had approved $250,000 for the new courthouse; the final bill was approximately $12 million, of which at least three-quarters was graft, funneled by means of fraudulent bills from contractors, plumbers, plasterers, furniture dealers and others into the hands of Tweed and his associates. The courthouse took so long to build, not for any inherent physical reason,

that it became a visible symbol to New Yorkers of the complete control exercised by Tammany Hall over the city's politics and finances. As the building finally neared completion, *Harper's*, which was waging a campaign against the Ring with the aid of the *New York Times* and others, commented: "The process seemed like the gradual upheaval of a continent, perceptible only by measurements separated by cycles. People who saw it every day forgot when it began, and at length came to regard it as something which had never had a beginning, and, probably, would never have an ending." It seems fitting that just as this view showing the finishing touches on his courthouse being completed was taken, Tweed and his group were on the verge of the first indictments and arrests which would eventually break the power of the Ring. (*Harper's Weekly*; September 9, 1871; drawn by Stanley Fox from a photograph by Rockwood.)

MR. TWEED'S WALKS WITH HIS PRIVATE SECRETARY.

MR. TWEED'S HEAD-QUARTERS.

THE WAY THE POOR FRIENDLESS CONVICT IS TREATED.

MR. TWEED'S SLEEPING-ROOM.

MR. TWEED'S DINING-HALL.

THE CELL IN WHICH THE POOR FRIENDLESS CONVICT SLEEPS.

TWEED IN PRISON, 1874 (Above). After Tweed's first trial ended in a hung jury, his second criminal trial resulted in his conviction in November, 1873. Following a reduction of the original 12-year sentence, he spent the period from the trial until January, 1875, in prison on Blackwell's (now Roosevelt) Island in the East River. In November, 1874 *Harper's* dispatched their artist, Theodore R. Davis, to sketch these scenes of Tweed's life in the penitentiary. The magazine reported that Tweed was not housed in the prison itself, but in the separate small building illustrated here. He slept in a large, well-furnished room, received visitors daily and occupied his time strolling around the grounds, entertaining friends and keeping up on his correspondence with the aid of his private secretary. The sketches here were intended to illustrate the differences in the lives led by Tweed and the "friendless convict" whose days were spent in tiny cells and at hard labor. *Harper's* disclosures of the way Tweed was being treated did not alter the situation. Rearrested on a civil action brought by the state in an attempt to recoup some of the money the Ring had stolen, Tweed found himself back in prison almost immediately after his release when he was unable to raise the $3-million bail. Again treated leniently, Tweed escaped from his jailors late in 1875 during a visit to his home, and ultimately made his way to Spain disguised as a sailor. Identified there because of a Thomas Nast cartoon, he was returned to America in November, 1876. Tweed died in New York's Ludlow Street jail on April 12, 1878. (*Harper's Weekly*; November 14, 1874; Theodore R. Davis.) VICTORIA WOODHULL AND WOMEN'S SUFFRAGE, 1871 (Opposite, Top). By the 1870s the women's suffrage movement was well under way in New York, although decades would pass before its goals would be achieved. Here the notorious Victoria Woodhull (then in the midst of her long and active career as spiritualist, clairvoyant, radical publisher, stockbroker, free-love reformer and women's rights advocate) and five other women attempt to vote on election day in 1871. She and her sister, Tennie Claflin, were unable to convince the Democratic inspector to receive their votes, although *Harper's* reported that the Republican inspector at this polling-place was willing to do so. One woman in the group, an otherwise unidentified Mrs. Miller, apparently succeeded in voting and boasted afterwards that she had cast her ballot for the Tweed ticket—leading some New York editorial writers to question even more the wisdom of granting women the right to vote. (*Harper's Weekly*; November 25, 1871; H. Balling.) A POLITICIAN'S NEW YEAR'S DAY RECEPTION, 1872 (Opposite, Bottom). A typical New Year's Day reception at the home of a Tammany Hall politician. *Harper's*, arch foe of Tammany, no doubt enjoyed publishing this little cartoon which they claimed accurately characterized the discomfiture of a Tammany Hall leader and his wife as they are obliged to receive, in the presence of elegant and somewhat disdainful guests, lower-class callers upon whose support their positions depend. "The majority [of the politician's guests] are of the lowest order, comprising pugilists, rum-sellers, ballot-box stuffers, election repeaters, corner loafers, and even common thieves. Men . . . venture to call who would not dare to show themselves at the basement door of the same house on any other day." (*Harper's Weekly*; February 10, 1872; W. J. Hennessy.)

A DEMOCRATIC BARBECUE, 1884. Democrats and their guests enjoying a Tammany Hall-sponsored roast at a political barbecue in Harlem. (*Frank Leslie's*; October 18, 1884.)

DEMONSTRATION IN UNION SQUARE, 1884. Union Square during a Democratic Party demonstration sponsored by Tammany Hall during the Presidential campaign of 1884. A crowd of 30,000 filled the square for several hours to hear speeches and watch the parades and fireworks. The display generated enthusiasm which evidently contributed to Grover Cleveland's election that November. The equestrian statue of George Washington by H. K. Brown and J. Q. A. Ward, a feature of Union Square since 1856, has since been moved to the center of the park. (*Frank Leslie's;* November 1, 1884.)

GROVER CLEVELAND CAMPAIGNING IN BROOKLYN, 1884. New York's Governor Grover Cleveland (raising his hat in the open carriage on the right) rides past Brooklyn's City Hall (now Borough Hall) at Fulton and Court Streets in October, 1884 en route to a large reception and barbe- cue at Ridgewood Park during the last part of his successful Presidential campaign. Borough Hall was completed in 1851. The Brooklyn Court House is in the background on the left. (*Harper's Weekly*; October 25, 1884; Schell & Hogan.)

DEMOCRATS AT MADISON SQUARE GARDEN, 1888. A view of the first Madison Square Garden building on the block bounded by Madison and Fourth Avenues and 26th and 27th Streets in 1888. A political meeting was being held in honor of Democratic Vice-Presidential candidate Allen G. Thurman, who was defeated along with President Cleveland that fall. This, the first Madison Square Garden, was adapted from railroad sheds leased by P. T. Barnum from Commodore Vanderbilt in 1873. First called the Great Roman Hippodrome, and then Gilmore's Garden, the building was finally named Madison Square Garden in 1879 when it was taken over by the son of the Commodore, William H. Vanderbilt. Boxing and other entertainments were held there during the 1880s. At the end of the decade the first Madison Square Garden was demolished to make way for McKim, Mead & White's elegant second Garden, which opened in 1890. (*Harper's Weekly*; September 15, 1888.)

MADISON SQUARE ON ELECTION NIGHT, 1888 (Above). Ten to fifteen thousand New Yorkers filled Madison Square until long past midnight to wait for returns. The illuminated messages flashed to the crowd on the *Herald*'s projection device shown here gave the early lead to Cleveland (the favorite in Democratic New York) but the final victory to Benjamin Harrison. This view is of the south end of the square; the message-screen was erected on a small building which occupied the triangular site at the intersection of Fifth Avenue, Broadway and 23rd Street until the Fuller "Flatiron" building went up there in 1902. As *Harper's* summed it up simply, "The Republicans went home happy." The building at the left is the Hotel Bartholdi, a favored stop with William Jennings Bryan. The American Art Galleries occupied space in it before it moved uptown and became part of Parke-Bernet. (*Harper's Weekly*; November 17, 1888; Charles Graham.) "STOP THIEF!" 1868 (Opposite, Top). A policeman chases a thief through a busy neighborhood. (*Harper's Weekly*; October 31, 1868.) STREETCAR TRAVEL, 1871 (Opposite, Bottom). The city's police were frequently under attack during

the century. In 1871 a man named Putnam was murdered on a Broadway streetcar, having protested when the woman he was with had been insulted by an unsavory character. *Harper's*, blaming such incidents on the Tweed Ring's dependence on lower-class support and the Ring's apathy toward such crimes and criminals (whose votes came in handy on election day), published this sketch entitled "Beauties of Streetcar Travel in New York" with the caption: "The sketch we give of a car crowded with murderers and thieves is a sight to be witnessed every day at almost every hour in New York. Many of the conductors and drivers are either in league with these ruffians' or so cowed by them as to be incapable of protecting their passengers from frequent insult and outrage." While this was a strong statement made in anger over one incident, there is no doubt that such incidents had increased in frequency during the century; New Yorkers certainly felt far less secure in the streets in 1871 than they had a generation before. (*Harper's Weekly*; May 20, 1871; drawn by C. S. Reinhart from a sketch by M. Woolf.)

THE MOUNTED POLICE, 1873 (Top). In 1873 New York had 34 mounted policemen divided into two squads. One squad of 18 was stationed at Carmansville, a village in upper Manhattan, which was still relatively sparsely populated; their main job was to patrol between Harlem and Yonkers on the lookout for highway robbers, housebreakers and fires. The other squad of 16 men was stationed at Eighth Avenue and 31st Street; their main concern was the prevention of dangerously fast driving of horses and wagons and theft of wagons on the West Side avenues. (*Harper's Weekly*; February 15, 1873; Frank Bellew.) DORMITORY FOR LOST CHILDREN, 1875 (Bottom). A scene at police headquarters on Mulberry Street.

(*Frank Leslie's*; September 11, 1875.) SHOOTING A MAD DOG, 1879 (Opposite, Top). A policeman shoots a mad dog on a New York street during a summer heat wave in 1879. (*Harper's Weekly*; August 2, 1879; drawn by Ivan Pranishnikoff from a sketch by S. D. Ehrhart.) THE POLICE PARADE, 1885 (Opposite, Bottom). In the annual parade of the New York Police Department on May 27, 1885, 1400 officers, half the force, marched or rode up Broadway to the music of their band and the cheers of New Yorkers. In 1884 the city's police had made 70,000 arrests, which *Harper's*, in the post-Tweed era, considered a good return on the police budget of $3.5 million. (*Harper's Weekly*; June 6, 1885; T. de Thulstrup.)

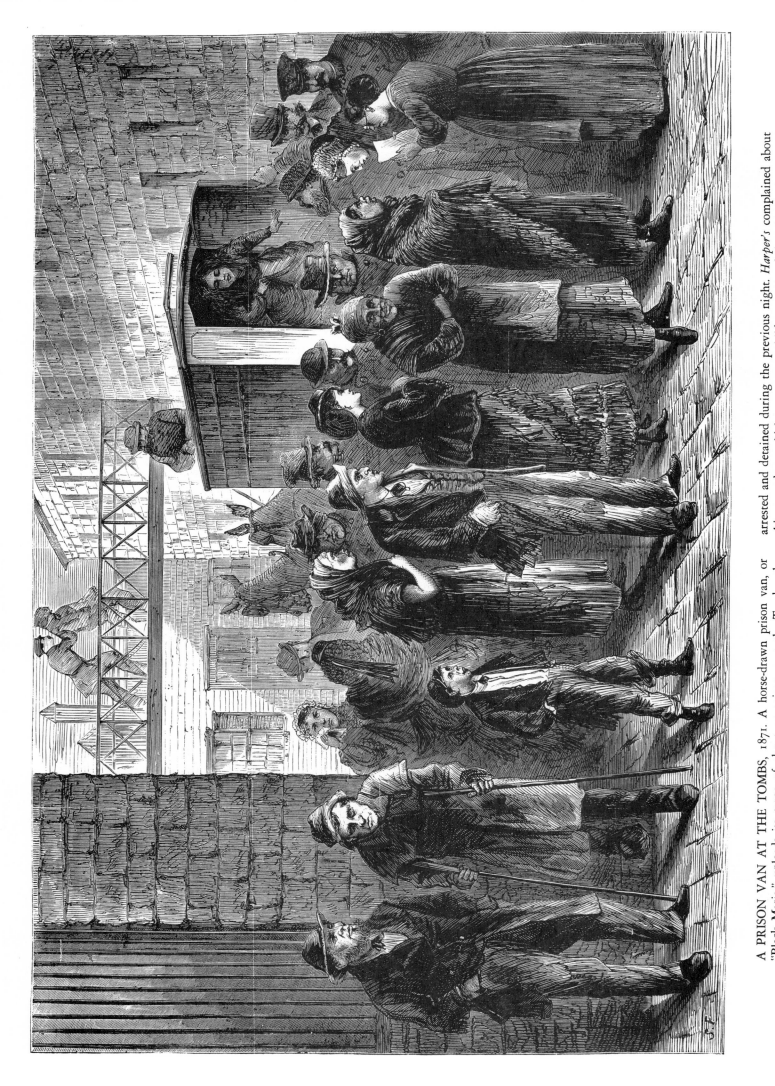

A PRISON VAN AT THE TOMBS, 1871. A horse-drawn prison van, or "Black Maria," unloads its cargo of about 25 prisoners at the Tombs, the city's main prison at Leonard and Centre Streets. Every morning the prison vans would go to the various police stations and pick up all who had been arrested and detained during the previous night. *Harper's* complained about this procedure, which saw young children, arrested for petty offenses and soon to be released, thrown together with hardened criminals. (*Harper's Weekly*; November 4, 1871; Stanley Fox.)

VISITING PRISONERS IN THE TOMBS, 1870 (Left). (*Harper's Weekly;* May 7, 1870.) AT THE TOMBS, 1871 (Right). A view of the prison pen in the Tombs. Every night, street vagrants, persons who had committed no crime other than having no place to go, were kept there until released or called for by a relative. (*Harper's Weekly;* February 18, 1871.)

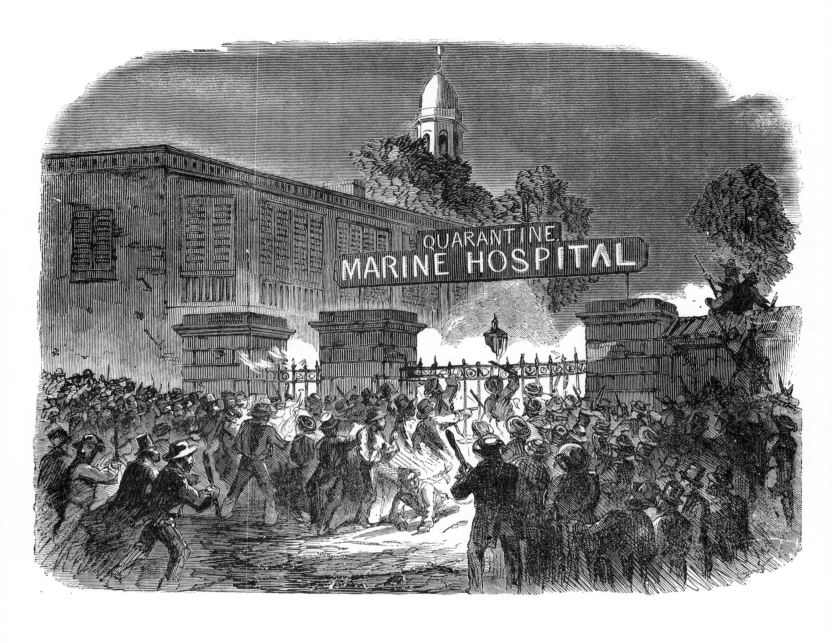

ATTACK ON THE QUARANTINE HOSPITAL, 1858. On the night of September 1, 1858, a mob of Staten Islanders, knowing that the city authorities would be preoccupied with the Atlantic Cable celebration then in progress at the Metropolitan Hotel, attacked and burned many of the buildings of the Quarantine Hospital, where yellow fever victims were cared for. Feelings against the hospital were strong because, although it was one of the leading facilities in the country for the treatment of yellow fever, its presence was blamed for the periodic outbreaks of the disease in the city, one of which had occurred that summer. The following night the mob returned and finished the job, this time including the principal hospital building itself. The patients were dragged out and left lying on the grass while the entire complex was burned to the ground. Local firemen did not interfere and it was rumored that the mob, shown here during the first night's attack, included a number of prominent citizens. Only after the fires were out did the state militia arrive; a few arrests were made but the instigators of the attack were never prosecuted. It is not unreasonable to suppose that the leaders of the draft riots five years later drew a lesson from the easy success of this mob action. (*Harper's Weekly*; September 11, 1858.)

ATTACK ON THE ORANGE SOCIETIES PARADE, 1871. One of the worst riots in New York's history occurred on July 12, 1871, when a procession of the Orange Societies, comprised of Protestant Irishmen, were attacked by a mob of Catholic Irishmen as they marched in commemoration of William of Orange's victory over the army of James II at the Battle of the Boyne on July 1, 1690. At the end of the riot 44 civilians, two soldiers and one policeman were dead and dozens more were injured on both sides. The passions aroused in New York by this traditional commemoration of a phase of the long struggle between Irish Protestants and Catholics understandably ran very high a century ago, when New York had just absorbed a large wave of Irish immigration. The traditional July 12 procession had been a cause of alarm before; only the previous year a few people had been killed in sporadic fighting and attempts were made to ban the 1871 procession altogether. However, after much complicated political infighting (the Irish Catholic community had the support of Tammany Hall in trying to have the parade banned) the parade was held with a military and police escort as we see in this view of Eighth Avenue between 24th and 25th Streets, the spot where the major action of the day occurred. Soldiers lead the procession, the head of the Orangemen follows on horseback in front of a banner with the portrait of William III. The hostile mob breaking in from the right is held off by the police while others fire from the windows and rooftops of buildings along the avenue. Most of the casualties occurred when the soldiers fired into the mob after the police line proved too weak. *Harper's* blamed Tammany Hall for not restraining the Catholic element, though a hardening of attitudes on both sides made the conflict (which no one seems to have tried very hard to prevent) almost inevitable. The sketch for this engraving was made on the scene by an unnamed soldier of New York's Seventh Regiment. (*Harper's Weekly*; July 29, 1871.)

A STREET RAILROAD STRIKE, 1886. A brief strike of the city's horse-car drivers, conductors and stable men led to a confrontation in the streets when the streetcar company attempted to drive one of the Grand Street cars along its usual route with a police escort. The drive was purely symbolic; company employees acted as driver, conductor and passengers. Despite the huge crowd of angry protestors who threw eggs and bricks and piled up heaps of debris along the route, the police succeeded in finally clearing the way for this one car. The total shutdown of the city's streetcar lines which followed was resolved only after negotiations gave the 15,000 workers what they considered a satisfactory settlement—two dollars a day for twelve hours of work with half an hour off for dinner. (*Harper's Weekly*, March 13, 1886; T. de Thulstrup.)

RIOT ON 42ND STREET NEAR BROADWAY, 1889 (Top). Streetcar operators went on strike again in 1889. The basic issue was recognition of the workmen's organization as well as wages and hours. Six thousand workmen went out on strike, bringing the city's transportation system to a standstill. Peace was restored only after a number of clashes such as this one, in which striking workmen tried to stop the companies' attempts to operate the streetcars. (*Harper's Weekly*; February 9, 1889; Graham & Durkin.) STARTING A STREETCAR ON SIXTH AVENUE, 1889 (Bottom). Another incident during the strike of 1889. (*Harper's Weekly*; February 9, 1889; W. P. Snyder.)

PARADE OF THE FIRE DEPARTMENT, 1866 (Top). The colorful career of New York City's Volunteer Fire Department came to an end with the creation of the professional Metropolitan Fire Department at a time when the city had grown too big, and the responsibility for fire protection too great, to be entrusted to amateur volunteers, no matter how gallant and enthusiastic they had been in the past. Members of the Paid Department, as it was popularly called, are seen here marching with their equipment in Maiden Lane in the Department's Second Annual Parade, late in 1866. From Fire Commissioner John Abbé's speech after the parade come many details of the Department's organization at that time. Below 83rd Street, the Department had 34 steam engines and 12 hook and ladder trucks with 12 men for each piece of equipment—a total of 552 men on the payroll, 138 of whom were constantly on patrol. The Department included 130 horses, each of which stood hitched to his equip-

ment and ready to move for 12 of every 24 hours; the men, each with one free day in twelve, had less time off than the horses. Regulations called for each fire company to be rolling within 40 seconds of receiving an alarm, and several companies made it consistently in 25 seconds. Boilers were kept hot constantly so that steam power for spraying water would always be available. The city was divided into eleven fire districts and all the fire houses were connected with each other and with the police stations and a central office by telegraph. (*Harper's Weekly*; December 8, 1866; A. R. Waud.) RUNNING TO A FIRE, 1872 (Bottom). A cartoon published by *Harper's* (with claims that it was not exaggerated) shows the consequences of the firemen's eagerness in responding to alarms. The paper was glad to report that the new Paid Fire Department was proving to be vastly superior to the earlier volunteers. (*Harper's Weekly*; February 24, 1872; Thomas Worth.)

STORAGE ROOM

SAVING GOODS

AT A FIRE.

BUNK ROOM.

THE FIRE INSURANCE PATROL, 1876. The Fire Insurance Patrol had been organized by the city's major insurance companies. When a fire alarm was received, the men of the Insurance Patrol both assisted the city's regular firemen in trying to put it out, and then went about their real function: to protect property which might otherwise be damaged by water and smoke.

The Patrol operated from three buildings. The one shown in this picture, with men scrambling to answer an alarm in the middle of the night, was at No. 41 Murray Street. (*Harper's Weekly;* March 4, 1876; Ivan Pranishnikoff.)

BARNUM'S MUSEUM AFTER THE FIRE, 1868 (Top). The spectacular aftermath of a famous New York fire. Barnum's second Museum opened on Broadway in November, 1865. Less than two and a half years later, on the night of March 2, 1868, the new museum burned, as had the first, almost totally destroying the building and causing the deaths of most of the animals on display there. As the fire occurred on one of the coldest nights of the year, water from the firemen's hoses froze as soon as it hit the walls, forming the display of gigantic icicles illustrated here. (*Harper's Weekly*; March 21, 1868; Stanley Fox.) THE BURNING OF BARNUM'S HIP-

PODROME, 1873 (Bottom). Fire continued to dog Barnum's career. The showman inaugurated a new Hippodrome on Fourteenth Street in November, 1872. Only a month later the entire building was destroyed in this fire, which only two elephants and a camel survived. The indomitable Barnum immediately cabled his European agents to spend half a million dollars buying up new attractions; by April, 1874, he was on the road with another huge traveling show of animals and curiosities. (*Harper's Weekly*; January 11, 1873; from a photograph by Rockwood.)

THE BROOKLYN THEATRE FIRE, 1876. The burning of the Brooklyn Theatre on Washington Street was the worst fire in terms of loss of life that has ever occurred in the Greater New York area. On the night of December 5, 1876 actresses Kate Claxton and Maude Harrison were appearing in the title roles of *The Two Orphans* when, only minutes before the end of the play, a piece of scenery caught fire from a kerosene lamp. The orchestra was quickly emptied, but hundreds of spectators in the upper galleries panicked, jamming the single small staircase leading to the main floor so that most were trapped when, less than half an hour after the fire had started, the roof and walls collapsed upon them. Not until the following morning as firemen, who thought that most of the audience had escaped, started sifting through the rubble, was the extent of the disaster known. Exact figures were never determined, but it is certain that 289—possibly as many as 400—had been killed, including actors Claude Burroughs and H. S. Murdoch. The rest of the cast escaped; Kate Claxton was found the following morning, in shock and badly burned, walking in Manhattan's City Hall Park with no recollection of how she had crossed the river from Brooklyn. (*Harper's Weekly*; December 23, 1876; Granville Perkins.)

THE BROOKLYN THEATRE FIRE: IDENTIFYING VICTIMS, 1876 (Opposite, Top). Bodies of the victims of the fire were laid out in the Adams Street market house on the night after the disaster, each one with a candle to assist in the difficult process of identification. (*Frank Leslie's*; December 23, 1876.) THE BROOKLYN THEATRE FIRE: BURIAL OF UNCLAIMED DEAD, 1876 (Opposite, Bottom). A great many of the bodies of the victims of the Brooklyn Theatre Fire were burned beyond recognition. About 100 unclaimed and unidentifiable corpses were buried in a common grave in Brooklyn's Greenwood Cemetery a few days after the disaster. (*Harper's Weekly*; December 30, 1876; E. A. Abbey.) A FACTORY FIRE, 1888 (Above). Firemen at work during a fire at the Potter and Stymus Co. furniture factory on Lexington Avenue between 41st and 42nd Streets. (*Harper's Weekly*; March 10, 1888; F. V. Du Mond.)

FIRE ENGINE EXPLOSION, 1868. The new steam fire engines developed around the middle of the century were a vast improvement over earlier hand-powered models, but they sometimes malfunctioned with disastrous results. On the evening of June 18, Fire Company No. 9 from East Broadway was called to a fire opposite the Bowery Theatre where a large audience was watching a performance of *Henry Dunbar; Or, A Daughter's Trial*. The fire was put out without difficulty but just as the theater crowd went into the street during an intermission, the boiler of this steam fire engine exploded, hurling scalding water and metal fragments in the air over a wide area. The disaster left five dead and 22 injured. (*Frank Leslie's*; July 4, 1868.)

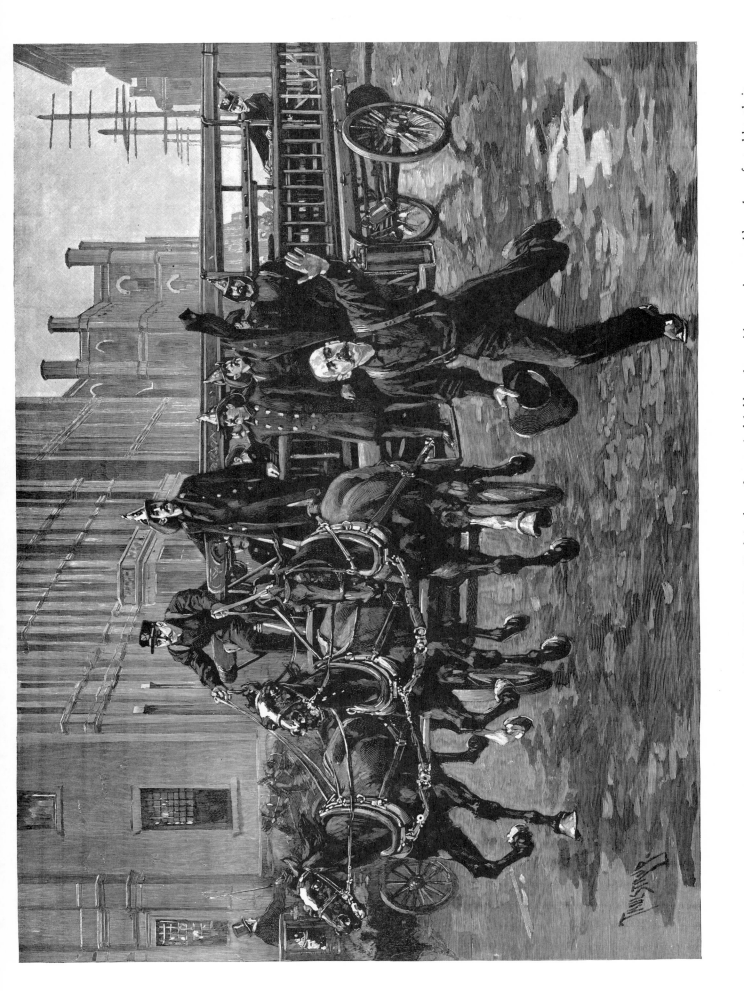

A HOOK AND LADDER COMPANY ON THE RUN. A New York hook and ladder company starts out for a fire. The fireman running beside the horses is warning other drivers to clear the way. By this time the city's firemen had ladders that, with extensions, could reach 90 feet although in the skyscraper age just beginning these would prove very inadequate. (*Harper's Weekly*, March 7, 1891; T. de Thulstrup.)

MAILMEN, 1868. A group of the city's mail carriers off to deliver their letters in new uniforms. (*Harper's Weekly*; December 26, 1868; Paul Frenzeny.)

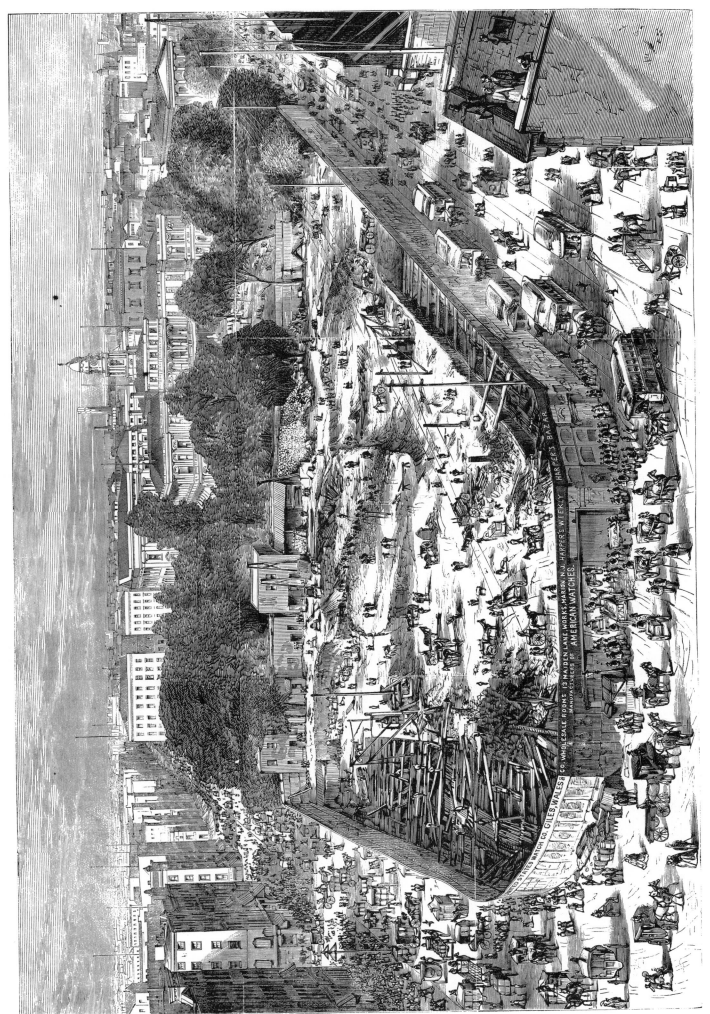

BUILDING THE NEW POST OFFICE, 1869. An unusual view of excavation under way for construction of the new main city Post Office at the southern end of City Hall Park. Broadway is at the left; Park Row is on the right; City Hall is seen just to the north of the building site with the Hall of Records on its eastern side. The Post Office, designed in a Neo-Renaissance style by government architect A. B. Mullett, who also built the Navy, War and State Department buildings in Washington, D.C., was completed in 1875. (*Harper's Weekly*, October 23, 1869; from a photograph by Rockwood.)

THE NEW POST OFFICE BUILDING AFTER COMPLETION, 1875 (Top). Inadequate in facilities virtually from the day it was opened, and considered an eyesore, the building was demolished in 1938–39 after the new main Post Office had been constructed at its present location on Eighth Avenue near Penn Station. Road construction and an extension of City Hall Park have since covered the site. The street scene depicted here seems to justify the claim of many writers that this area had most of the city's busiest intersections throughout the century. (*Frank Leslie's*; September 18, 1875.)

PARADE OF POST OFFICE CLERKS, 1875 (Bottom). Postal clerks celebrating their departure from the old post office in the Middle Dutch Church building on Nassau Street for the new building at the foot of City Hall Park. (*Frank Leslie's*; September 18, 1875.)

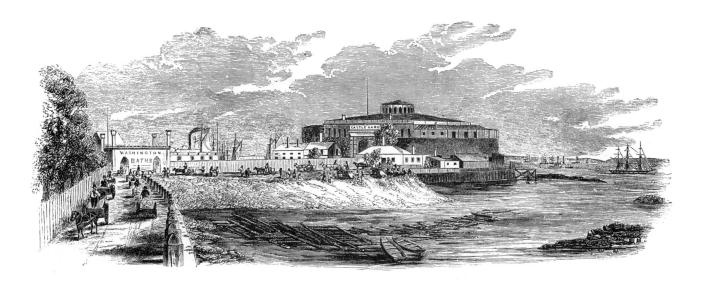

CASTLE GARDEN AND THE BATTERY, 1853 (Top). Castle Garden was originally a fort, the West Battery (later named Castle Clinton), built on a pile of rocks off the Battery in 1807, when relations with England were deteriorating. Taken over by the City in 1824, it was renamed Castle Garden. The fort was roofed over and opened as a concert hall in 1845; it was there that Jenny Lind made her American debut under the aegis of P. T. Barnum on September 11, 1850. In 1855 Castle Garden was again converted; this time into an immigration depot when existing facilities had been overwhelmed by the flood of new settlers. For 40 years Castle Garden served as New York's immigration center; 7.5 million newcomers to America, at first primarily from Ireland and Germany, later from Eastern and Southern Europe as well, passed through its doors. Supplanted by Ellis Island in the 1890s, Castle Garden was transformed into an aquarium which operated there until 1941. In 1946 its exterior was restored to something like its original condition and it was made a national historic monument. Its interior has since been restored and the building is now open to the public. This view shows Castle Garden and the Battery from the west in 1853, as work was under way to enlarge the Battery to its present size. Wagons brought coal ashes, construction scrap and miscellaneous rubbish to use as landfill. When the project was finished in 1868, the area of the Battery had been increased from 10 to 24 acres and the length of the sea wall from 1620 to 2120 feet. In the process Castle Garden, which had previously been joined to the mainland by a 300-foot bridge, was surrounded, becoming a part of Battery Park. On the left in this view are the entrances to the floating baths which flourished at the Battery throughout the century. (*Illustrated News*; July 23, 1853.) THE LABOR EXCHANGE AT CASTLE GARDEN, 1868 (Bottom). The Labor Exchange was an attempt to provide as many immigrants as possible with legitimate employment on their arrival in New York. Previously the unschooled immigrants had been easy prey for swindlers. At the Labor Exchange, only reputable employers could file requests for laborers, domestic servants, cooks, etc., and the Exchange attempted to match the requests with the available supply. Farm laborers and domestic servants were paid $6–$10 a month plus room and board and trained cooks received a bit more. Often whole families were hired together. In the first six months of 1868 alone, 13,000 men and women were placed by the Exchange, which received no commissions for its work. This illustration depicts immigrants being interviewed by prospective employers inside the building. (*Harper's Weekly*; August 15, 1868; Stanley Fox.)

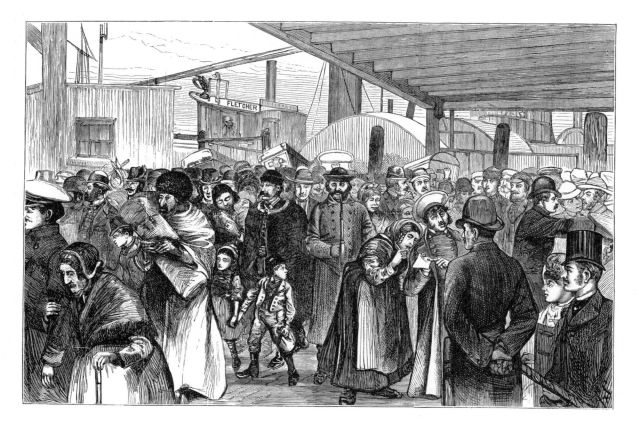

ON THE BATTERY, 1878 (Top). Immigrants promenading on the Battery near Castle Garden on a spring evening. The shiploads of immigrants arriving daily at Castle Garden presented great contrasts between those arriving with enough money to take them to the West immediately, where they would purchase farms and those at the other end of the scale who would soon swell the ranks of New York's poor. (*Harper's Weekly*; April 6, 1878; E. A. Abbey.)

LANDING AT CASTLE GARDEN, 1880 (Bottom). When this group of immigrants at Castle Garden was drawn in 1880, the flow of immigration was again on the rise after a decline during the depression of the mid-1870s. Forty percent of the 180,000 immigrants who arrived in 1879 remained in the East; the majority of those who went West settled in Minnesota, Illinois, Wisconsin and Missouri. (*Harper's Weekly*; May 29, 1880; A. B. Shults.)

EXAMINATION OF STEERAGE PASSENGERS, 1887 (Top). In the second half of the nineteenth century, during the high tide of European immigration, all ships entering New York were held at Quarantine Point in the Bay near Staten Island while health officers examined them for signs of the century's dread diseases—yellow fever, cholera, typhus and smallpox. A ship bearing a clean bill of health, a certificate signed by the American consul in the port from which it came certifying that there had been no disease there, and whose Captain was prepared to swear that there was no disease on board, might not have its passengers examined individually. A ship without a clean bill would be held while a squad of health officers, headquartered at Quarantine Point, boarded it for examination. If necessary, they could hospitalize the passengers and fumigate both ship and cargo with steam before permitting the ship to land. At this time there was a floating hospital in the Bay and two quarantine hospitals on Swinburne and Hoffman Islands, also in the Bay. (*Harper's Weekly*; October 8, 1887; A. Berghaus.) AN IMMIGRANT WAGON, 1873 (Bottom). A scene frequently witnessed on the streets of New York during the second half of the century—a procession of immigrants on their way either directly from Castle Garden or from a boardinghouse to the trains which will take them to their new homes, most likely in the West. (*Harper's Weekly*; October 25, 1873; Frenzeny & Tavernier.)

DEPARTING FOR THE WEST, 1871 (Top). While many immigrants settled in New York, the vast majority of them only passed through the city on their way to farms, cities and towns in the rest of the country. *Harper's* claimed that a scene such as this could be witnessed *every* evening at the railroad depot at Varick and Beach Streets where immigrants, primarily Germans at this time but with a mixture of other nationalities, went to board trains for the West. (*Harper's Weekly*; September 2, 1871; W. L. Sheppard.) SECUR-

ING CERTIFICATES OF NATURALIZATION, 1868 (Bottom). Immigrants becoming naturalized citizens at New York's City Hall in 1868, just weeks before the election which saw Grant succeed to the Presidency. *Harper's*, which was always Republican, often commented caustically on the ease with which the city's Democratic organization, Tammany Hall, was able to cut through red tape to produce new voters at election time with assembly-line efficiency. (*Harper's Weekly*; October 10, 1868; Stanley Fox.)

STREET PEDDLERS BEFORE THE COMMISSIONERS OF CHARITY, 1869 (Top). In 1869 the police arrested vagrant children who earned their meagre living by selling cigars, buttons, matches and similar articles on the city's streets and sent them to the homes for orphans and abandoned children on Randall's Island. *Harper's* published this scene of some of the children being brought before the Commissioners of Charity. Thousands of New York's abandoned children populated the Randall's Island homes, where they were given a rudimentary education and eventually apprenticed to various trades, but thousands more continued to roam the city's streets. (*Harper's Weekly*; January 30, 1869; Paul Frenzeny.) DISTRIBUTION OF COAL TO THE POOR, 1877 (Bottom). Money for charity was not plentiful during the winter of 1877 and private charitable organizations, such as St. John's Guild, were sorely pressed by the number of applicants for funds with which to purchase food. The city did help by distributing a quantity of free coal to the poor. This engraving is of a scene in Cherry Street, where the coal was put out to be carried away by those who needed it. (*Harper's Weekly*; March 10, 1877; C. A. Keetels.)

THE RANDALL'S ISLAND POORHOUSE, 1875 (Above). A line of men wait in the snow for dinner at the poorhouse on Randall's Island in the East River. (*Frank Leslie's*; February 13, 1875; Joseph Becker.) COOPER UNION, 1861 (Opposite, Top). Cooper Union, one of the oldest free educational institutions in the country, was opened in 1859 at what is now called Cooper Square, between Astor Place and Seventh Street. The brownstone Italianate building was designed by Frederick A. Petersen and financed by industrialist-philanthropist Peter Cooper, whose fortune had been made largely in the iron business. Some of Cooper's own iron is still present in the building although the structure has been considerably altered over the past century. A novel feature of the original design was the circular elevator shaft which Cooper had incorporated in the design although there was not as yet an elevator available on the market to fit it. With emphasis on the applied arts and design, Cooper Union

has had many distinguished graduates over the years, including Raphael Soyer and Augustus Saint-Gaudens, and was ahead of its time in opening its doors to women students from the beginning. The reading room, library and picture gallery were among the first in the city to be available to the general public, and the large auditorium, the Great Hall, was frequently used for public meetings and lectures. Abraham Lincoln's memorable speech there on February 27, 1860 served to launch his Presidential campaign, helping to transform the candidate from an unknown Western lawyer into the leading Republican contender. (*Harper's Weekly*; March 30, 1861.) THE MEDICAL COLLEGE FOR WOMEN, 1870 (Opposite, Bottom). The main dissecting room of the Medical College for Women on East 12th Street and Second Avenue. (*Frank Leslie's*; April 16, 1870; Albert Berghaus.)

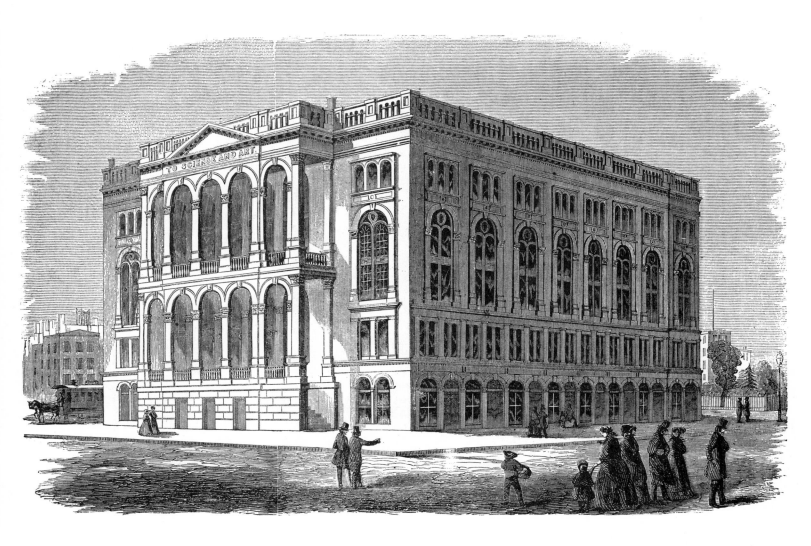

INTERIOR OF THE ASTOR LIBRARY, 1875 (Above). The Astor Library, the first free public library in New York, was built with a $400,000 bequest from the will of John Jacob Astor. The Italianate building on Lafayette Place (now Lafayette Street) was constructed over three decades by three different architects. The south wing was designed by Alexander Saeltzer and completed in 1854, when the library first opened. Between 1856 and 1859 Griffith Thomas built the center section, illustrated here, and Thomas Stent added the north wing in 1879–81. Of the original bequest, $120,000 was appropriated for books and many thousands of volumes were acquired in Europe by the library's first superintendent, J. G. Cogswell. By 1875 the collection numbered 150,000 volumes, making it the greatest library in America. In 1912 the Astor Library merged with the Lenox Library and the Tilden Foundation to form the nucleus of the New York Public Library at Fifth Avenue and 42nd Street. The Astor Library building then became the headquarters of the Hebrew Immigrant Aid Society. Narrowly avoiding demolition in the 1960s, the building was designated a landmark by the Landmarks Preservation Commission and now, after extensive interior remodelling by architect Giorgio Cavaglieri, it houses several auditoriums of the New York Shakespeare Festival. Despite the necessary alterations, much of the interior architecture seen in this view is still intact. (*Harper's Weekly*; October 2, 1875.) COLUMBIA COLLEGE, 1885 (Opposite). Columbia College's Hamilton Hall at Madison Avenue and 50th Street as it appeared five years after this new "Collegiate Gothic" building designed by Charles C. Haight had been added to Columbia's midtown campus. Founded as King's College in 1754, with eight students, Columbia (as it had been renamed in 1784) had moved uptown from its original site at Church Street and Park Place in 1857. When this view was drawn Columbia had a faculty of 114 and about 1500 students; the smaller views are of students at work in the laboratory of the new School of Mines, which had been added to the College in 1864, and a Greek Revival doorway of one of the older buildings on the midtown campus which *Harper's* editors felt contrasted nicely with the "modernity" of Hamilton Hall. Despite the Victorian solidity of the new structure, Columbia did not remain midtown much longer; a decade later the still growing College established itself on its present site on Morningside Heights. (*Harper's Weekly*; June 20, 1885; Schell & Hogan.)

SCHOOL OF MINES.

A BIT OF OLD & NEW.

THE COLUMBIA COLLEGE CANE RUSH, 1882. Freshmen and sophomores from Columbia College enact the annual "cane rush," one of the rituals of college life, on the grounds of the New York Athletic Club at Mott Haven. It was traditional at Columbia that freshmen not carry canes on campus before the spring of their first year, under threat of attack from the upperclassmen should this prohibition be ignored. The only way around the rule was the "cane rush" held each fall. The two sides came together to fight over a cane, as seen in this engraving; whichever side had the most hands on the cane after fifteen minutes of general gouging, kicking and punching, won. If the freshmen won, they were allowed to carry canes before the spring. On this occasion, the sophomores won, eight hands to six, and the freshmen of 1882 were forbidden to carry their canes until the following spring. (*Frank Leslie's*; October 21, 1882.)

PUBLIC SCHOOLS, 1881. There were about 120,000 public school students in New York when this view was drawn of a class beginning the day with calisthenic exercises set to music—a new feature of the curriculum. (*Frank Leslie's*, September 17, 1881.)

MARKET INSPECTION, 1873 (Top). During the period before widespread refrigeration, the problem of spoiled and decayed food was considerable; spoiled food was responsible for many deaths every year. Here Board of Health inspectors clear the fruit stands in a small Manhattan grocery. New regulations were passed and spot inspections such as this were carried out often but it was impossible for the Board to maintain a meaningful watch on all the markets in the growing city. (*Harper's Weekly*; September 13, 1873; R. Lewis.) TAKING SMALLPOX VIRUS FROM A CALF, 1872 (Bottom).

Smallpox was a problem in 1872 both for the city as a whole and for the New York Dispensary (located at Centre and White Streets) which had undertaken to provide doctors with a steady supply of pure vaccine. The vaccine was obtained from calves by a physician who removed lymph, as shown here. None of the calves was ever used twice and we are told that maintaining a constant supply of fresh calves, which were kept in the country, presented many difficulties for the city's medical leaders to overcome. (*Harper's Weekly*; February 24, 1872; Stanley Fox.)

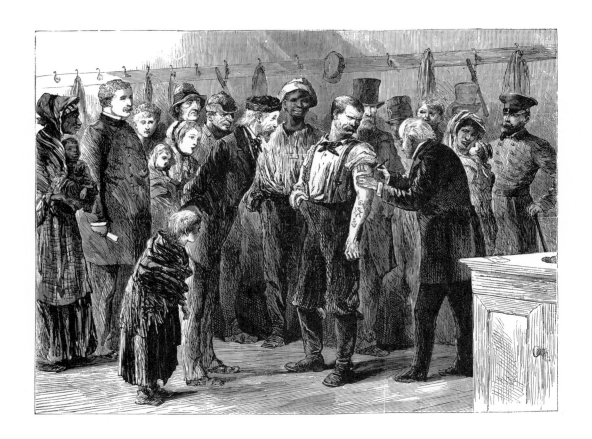

VACCINATING THE POOR, 1872 (Top). A typical scene in a New York police station during a smallpox epidemic in 1872. Under supervision of the Board of Health, poor people receive free vaccinations from physicians. (*Harper's Weekly*; March 16, 1872; Sol Eytinge, Jr.) THE NEW YORK EYE AND EAR INFIRMARY, 1875 (Bottom). A scene in the busy New York Eye and Ear Infirmary, established 1820. In 1875 it was located at Second Avenue and Thirteenth Street. (*Frank Leslie's*; April 10, 1875.)

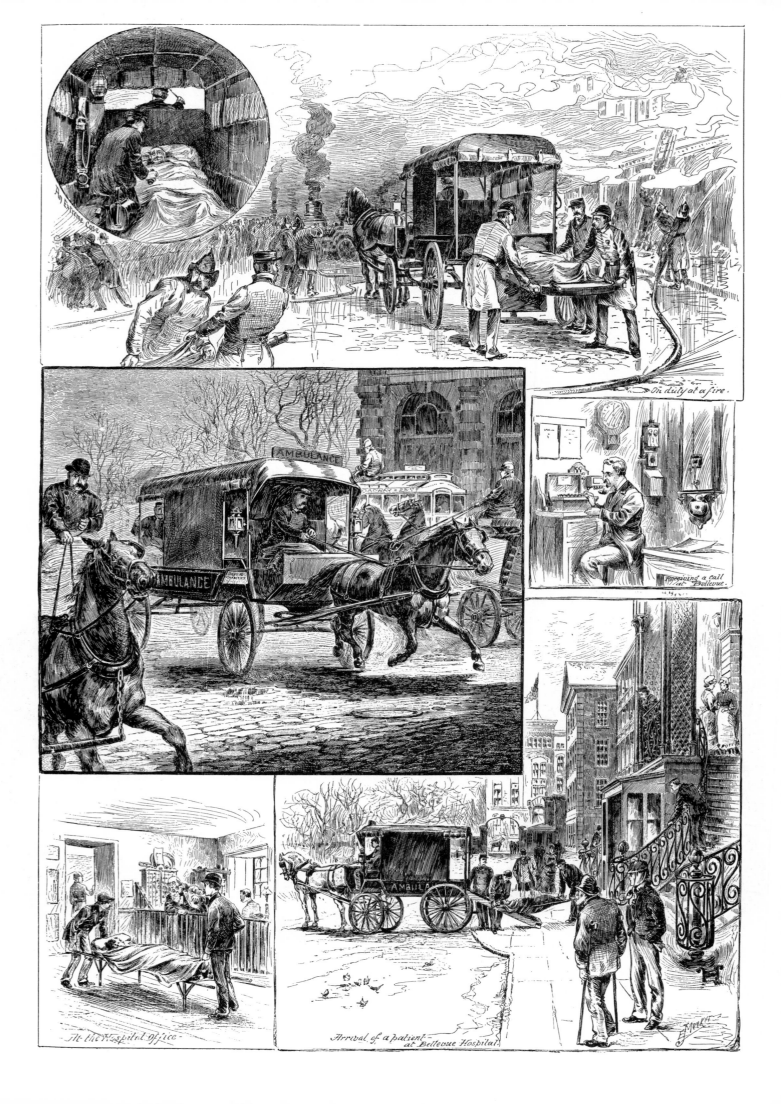

An Extreme Case.

On duty at a fire.

Receiving a call at Bellevue.

At the Hospital Office.

Arrival of a patient at Bellevue Hospital.

THE NEW YORK AMBULANCE SERVICE, 1884 (Opposite). In 1884, eight years after the New York Ambulance Service had begun operation, *Harper's* published this page of sketches of the horse-drawn ambulances receiving a patient at a fire and transporting him to Bellevue Hospital. At this time there were seven hospitals in New York which had ambulances—New York Hospital, the Church Street branch of the New York Hospital, St. Vincent's, Bellevue, the 99th Street branch of Bellevue, Presbyterian Hospital and Roosevelt Hospital. Like the fire engines, ambulances and their horses were kept ready around the clock. Traffic regulations gave the city's ambulances the right of way over all other traffic except that of the U.S. Mail and the Fire Department. Other drivers were used to moving out of an ambulance's way when its bells rang. (*Harper's Weekly*; May 24, 1884; E. Meeker.) THE METROPOLITAN BOARD OF HEALTH, 1866 (Top). The large and ever-increasing numbers of unskilled impoverished immigrants living in overcrowded, decaying tenements created problems which the resources of the city always proved inadequate to solve. Organized in 1805, the Metropolitan Board of Health tried to relieve conditions although they were often unequal to the task. *Harper's* credited the Board with effectively fighting cholera in the city, but there is no question that conditions in the tenements of the poor throughout the century were beyond anything that the city was willing or able to alleviate permanently. Here agents of the Board cart garbage away from a tenement. (*Harper's Weekly*; October 6, 1866; Stanley Fox.) CLEARING OUT A DIVE, 1873 (Bottom). The Sanitary Inspectors of the Board of Health held periodic drives to clean up "dives"—basements where dozens of people rented lodgings either in a common room or in tiny cubicles. The entire contents of this dive are being carried to the street to be thrown away. These vermin-infested basement lodgings were found in many parts of lower Manhattan; the drive of 1873 found the worst rooms on Mott Street, Mulberry Street and Madison Street. (*Harper's Weekly*; July 12, 1873; C. S. Reinhart.)

THE DISINFECTING CORPS, 1884 (Opposite, Top). Members of the Disinfecting Corps of New York's Health Department distribute disinfectant in a run-down neighborhood as part of the struggle against cholera which city officials waged continuously throughout the century. (*Frank Leslie's*; July 26, 1884.) THE MORGUE, 1866 (Opposite, Bottom). "It is astounding," wrote *Harper's*, "how many die in this city of whom absolutely nothing is known." New York was by this time developing into a city so vast that it would be as easy to die in it as to live in it with total anonymity. This situation presented certain difficulties for the authorities. Unidentified corpses had previously been sent without delay to Potter's Field for immediate burial, but in 1866 the city finally built a modern morgue, illustrated here, on the grounds of Bellevue Hospital at 26th Street on the East River where bodies could be kept while relatives or friends were advertised for. Corpses were kept as shown, in a cold, stone-walled room, their clothes hung beside them to assist in identification. A constant spray of water aided in preservation. The new morgue, which took its name from the one at Paris, was also used to keep identified bodies awaiting transportation, and the bodies of newborn children found around the city—a common occurrence in the nineteenth century. (*Harper's Weekly*; July 7, 1866; Stanley Fox.) THE START OF THE S.P.C.A., 1865 (Above). This newspaper illustration played a part in the history of nineteenth-century New York. The drawing of an overworked horse being beaten as spectators and a policeman stand idly by was seen by Henry Bergh and became one of the forces which motivated Bergh to found, after the English model, the Society for the Prevention of Cruelty to Animals. The drawing itself was adopted by Bergh for the seal of the Society. Son of a prominent New York shipbuilder, Bergh labored tirelessly for decades to promote the welfare of animals. He not only fought those who mistreated working animals, but took on sportsmen and upper-class New Yorkers who mistreated their animals. (It was, for example, the fashion to clip horses' coats so short that in winter the animals were uncomfortable on the cold city streets.) In a celebrated incident, Bergh criticized P. T. Barnum for having a circus horse jump through a flaming hoop; Barnum himself jumped through the hoop to prove it wasn't painful. Though his first concern was the city's animals, Bergh was also instrumental in establishing the Society for the Prevention of Cruelty to Children. (*Frank Leslie's*; October 28, 1865; Albert Berghaus.)

THE CROWDED CAR, 1872 (Top). Henry Bergh is seen at the right, stopping an overcrowded streetcar which is obviously too much for the two horses to pull. Scenes like this were common in New York where there were no legal limits on the number of passengers who might try to crowd themselves into the busy cars. *Harper's* pointed out that in Paris streetcars were only permitted to pick up as many passengers as there were seats available—an idea many New Yorkers could not quite understand. (*Harper's Weekly*; September 21, 1872; Sol Eytinge, Jr.) THE DOG POUND, 1883 (Bottom). (*Harper's Weekly*; June 16, 1883; W. A. Rogers.)

A HORSE AMBULANCE, 1888. The Society for the Prevention of Cruelty to Animals maintained two specially constructed ambulances for animals. Disabled and sick horses like this one could be lifted into them by means of a winch-driven sliding panel. The new ambulances occasionally had to lift and carry disabled circus elephants and other exotic beasts, a test which they passed with flying colors. (*Harper's Weekly*; January 14, 1888; W. P. Bodfish.)

THE SOCIETY FOR THE PREVENTION OF CRUELTY TO CHILDREN, 1882. The Society for the Prevention of Cruelty to Children was founded in New York in 1875 by Henry Bergh. Seven years after its founding, the Society, the first organization to provide any protection for abused children in the city, was handling thou-sands of complaints annually, removing children from unfit homes and prosecuting offenders through the courts. This melodramatic engraving represents the timely intervention of officers in a tenement. (*Frank Leslie's*; March 4, 1882.)

THE FULTON FISH MARKET, 1869 (Top). The Fulton Market, on the north side of Fulton Street between South and Front Streets, was built in 1821 and replaced by a new building in 1882. When this view was drawn, the wholesale fish business was thriving; the fourteen firms of the Fulton Market ran a fleet of 111 ships and annually sold well over $2 million worth of fish of all varieties—including both saltwater and freshwater fish brought from as far away as Canada and North Carolina. Terrapin was one of the gourmet delicacies of the period and figured prominently in many great dinners.

(*Harper's Weekly*; April 3, 1869; Stanley Fox.) OYSTER STANDS IN THE FULTON MARKET, 1870 (Bottom). Oysters, a prevalent delicacy of nineteenth-century New York, were sold in restaurants, bars and street stands throughout the city. This oyster stand at the Fulton Market counted among its lunchtime clientele many women who had spent the morning in the city's main shopping district on lower Broadway, not far from the East River waterfront and the Fulton Market. (*Harper's Weekly*; October 29, 1870; A. R. Waud.)

THE FULTON MARKET, 1875. "Ripe Watermelons—fine Savannahs, fresh and sweet! Only five cents a slice!" Eager customers crowd a stand at the market during the fruit season. (*Frank Leslie's*; September 4, 1875; Miranda.)

THE NEW FULTON MARKET, 1882 (Top). The Fulton Market's new building, designed by Douglas Smyth, drawn as it was nearing completion in 1882. This Victorian brick and terra-cotta structure survived until it was replaced by the present Fulton Market building in the 1950s. (*Harper's* *Weekly*; March 11, 1882; Charles Graham.) LANDING SLIP AT FULTON MARKET, 1887 (Bottom). A fleet of fishing boats unloading their fresh cargo at the Fulton Market. (*Harper's Weekly*; April 30, 1887; D. C. Beard.)

WASHINGTON MARKET, 1872. *Harper's* described Washington Market, which ran along the Hudson River from Fulton to Vesey Streets, and the Fulton Market as "collections of low straggling sheds divided into irregular lanes and stalls, where order is impossible and cleanliness nearly so." The description was accurate, as can be seen in this vivid view at Thanksgiving time, when market activity was most intense. The two markets were the centers from which New York bought meat, fish, vegetables and fruits, here displayed for buyers in hopeless disarray. (*Harper's Weekly*; November 30, 1872; Jules Tavernier.)

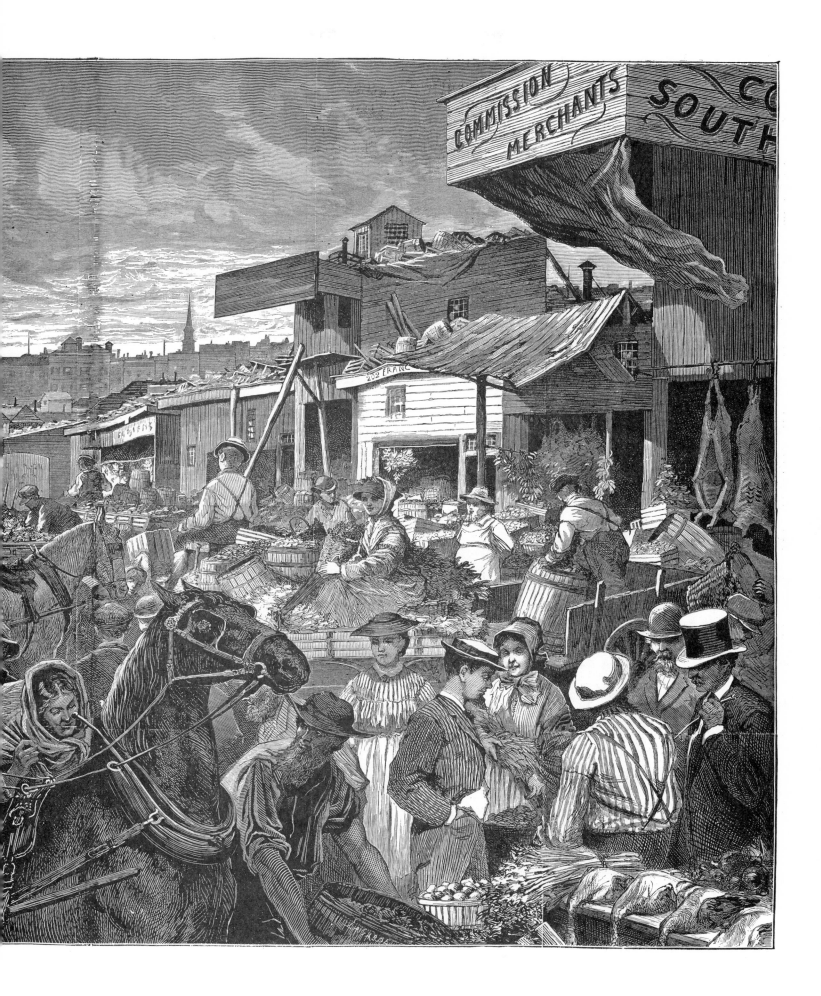

WASHINGTON MARKET, 1869 (Top). A view of part of Washington Market shows the truck-wagons in which produce was brought from the country each day. (*Harper's Weekly*; March 6, 1869; T. R. Davis.) WASHINGTON MARKET, 1884 (Bottom).

The opening of new buildings at the Washington Market was the occasion for this lively celebration by the men who worked there. (*Frank Leslie's*; December 27, 1884.)

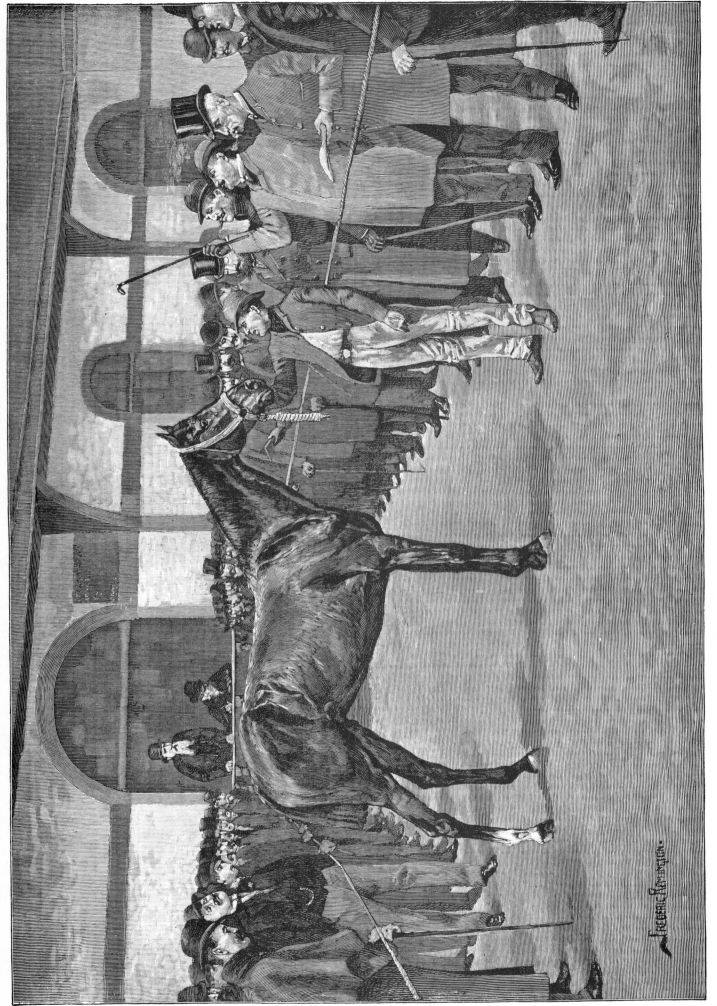

THE AMERICAN HORSE EXCHANGE, 1889. An auction sale of thoroughbred horses at the American Horse Exchange on Broadway at 50th Street was drawn by Frederic Remington, whose notable scenes of Western life were appearing regularly in *Harper's* at this time. The American Horse Exchange was the scene of frequent auction sales of horses from its opening in 1883 until it was demolished in 1910 to make way for the Schuberts' Winter Garden Theatre. At auctions such as this, a yearling with racing prospects might bring an average of from $2000 to $4000, a bit more than the trotting and fine carriage horses which were also sold at the Exchange. (*Harper's Weekly;* January 12, 1889; Frederic Remington.)

THE BULL'S HEAD HORSE MARKET, 1869. The Bull's Head Horse Market near Fifth Avenue and 46th Street. In contrast to the sales at the American Horse Exchange, sales of working horses were held regularly here for a city which depended on thousands of horses to maintain its daily life. (*Harper's Weekly*; February 13, 1869; A. R. Waud.)

SATURDAY NIGHT STREET MARKET ON NINTH AVENUE, 1890. Meat, poultry and produce are sold from truck-wagons at a Saturday night market on Ninth Avenue in 1890. Rather than hold perishable food over the weekend, New York's grocery merchants were allowed to dispose of the week's surplus on Saturday nights at this street market on Ninth Avenue between 34th and 42nd Streets and at a similar market on First Avenue just below 14th Street. Almost a century after this view was drawn, Ninth Avenue remains a market area. (*Harper's Weekly*, March 29, 1890; W. A. Rogers.)

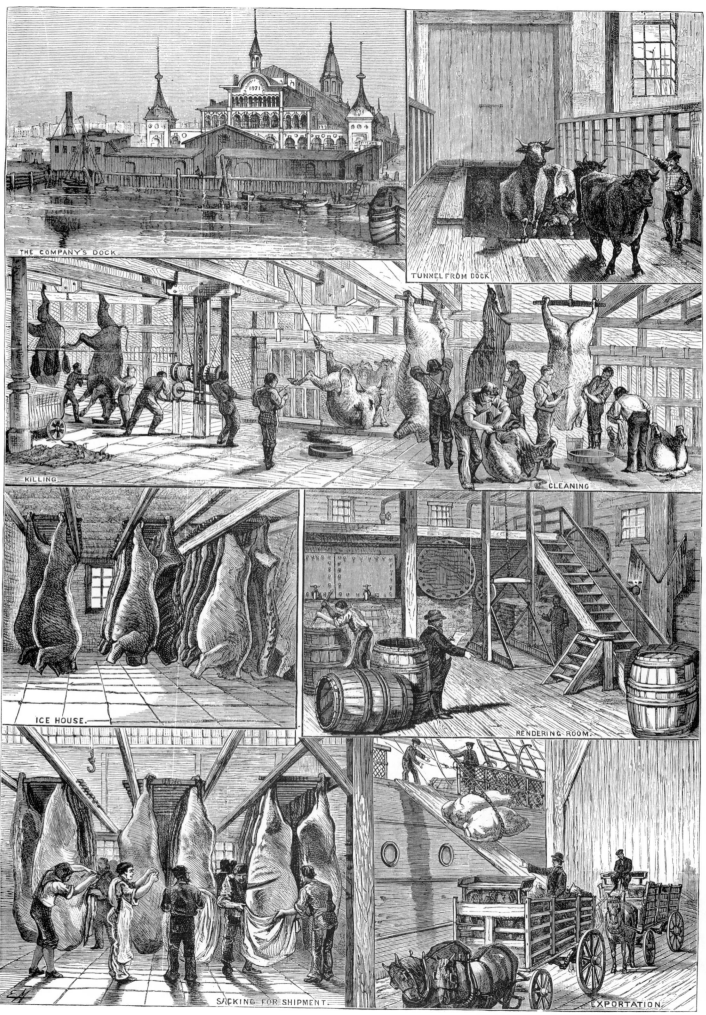

THE COMPANY'S DOCK.

TUNNEL FROM DOCK.

KILLING.

CLEANING.

ICE HOUSE.

RENDERING ROOM.

SACKING FOR SHIPMENT.

EXPORTATION.

THE MANHATTAN ABATTOIR, 1877 (Opposite). In 1877 New York and environs consumed about 10,000 head of cattle a week. This page of sketches of the slaughtering process at the Manhattan slaughterhouse, between Eleventh and Twelfth Avenues and 34th and 35th Streets, demonstrates the entire process from the time the cattle were landed on the Hudson River dock until their carcasses were sacked in canvas and ready for shipment to various markets. Cattle were first hoisted by their hind legs, then a butcher cut off their heads with two quick strokes of a short, sharp knife. Refrigeration was provided by large fans which circulated air cooled by huge blocks of ice. (*Harper's Weekly*; July 7, 1877; V. L. Kingsbury.)
BRADY'S DAGUERREOTYPE SALON, 1853 (Top). In the 1850s, Mathew B. Brady (later to achieve his greatest fame as a battlefield photographer of the Civil War) became one of the chief practitioners of one of fashionable New York's foremost pastimes— the taking of daguerreotypes. In his spacious, well-appointed rooms at No. 359 Broadway, near Barnum's American Museum, Brady and

his assistants received New Yorkers and no doubt tourists as well who came to try the new fad of having their picture taken. Brady's was the best-known of the many daguerreotype establishments on Broadway during this period. (*Illustrated News*; June 11, 1853).
THE SALESROOM OF HIRAM ANDERSON, 1853 (Bottom). This view shows the main-floor salesroom of Hiram Anderson at No. 99 The Bowery, where he advertised his business, selling both imported and American carpets, as the largest carpet establishment in the United States. At this time, the year of the opening of the Crystal Palace, American carpet making had advanced to the point where American manufacturing techniques were being copied extensively in England. Mentions of competition with English work figure in most contemporary discussions of American manufacturing; it was always a point of pride that native Americans felt they could do as well as, or better than, their British counterparts. (*Illustrated News*; November 12, 1853.)

PLACARD BEARERS, 1868 (Right). A few weeks after the previous illustration was published these placard bearers, including the man with the hand on his hat, were arrested by the police for causing a general nuisance and obstructing traffic on busy Broadway. (*Harper's Weekly;* March 21, 1868; R. Weir.)

BROADWAY, 1868 (Left). A fashionable crowd promenades in the shopping center of the city, the mile-long stretch of Broadway below 14th Street. A. T. Stewart's store at 10th Street and a host of other establishments catered to the needs of the city's middle and upper classes. The man in the right center, wearing a plaster glove on his hat, advertises a clothing firm. (*Harper's Weekly;* February 15, 1868; W. S. L. Jewett.) ARREST OF

A STREET AUCTION, 1868 (Top). Every spring the return of pleasant weather brought out the street auctioneers whose informal sales could be attended on many corners throughout the city. (*Harper's Weekly*; May 16, 1868; Stanley Fox.) A PICTURE AUCTION, 1875 (Bottom). Before there were the galleries and private dealers that dominate the art world today, auctions were by far the commonest means of disposing of the collection of a deceased (or bankrupt) collector. (*Frank Leslie's*; December 4, 1875; J. N. Hyde.)

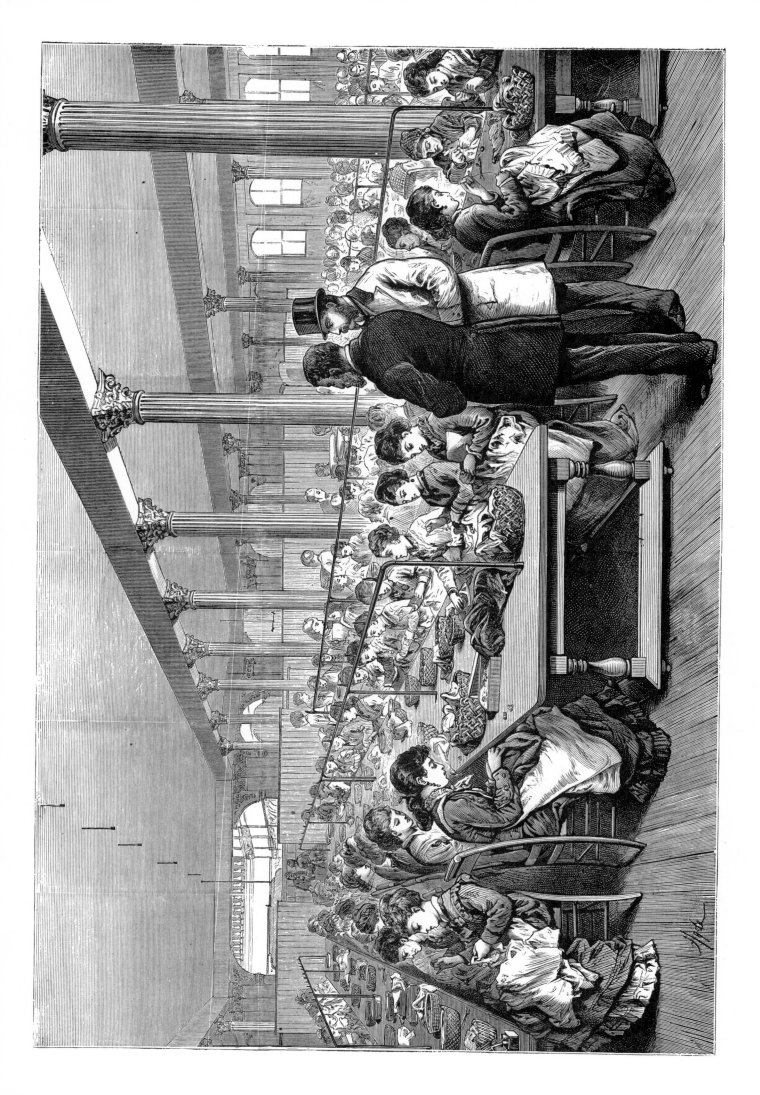

THE SEWING ROOM AT A. T. STEWART'S, 1875. Opened in 1859 on Broadway between 9th and 10th Streets, A. T. Stewart's department store was at the height of its popularity in 1875. Several hundred women were employed in sewing by hand the clothes sold at Stewart's. The store also specialized in selling the materials with which women could make their own clothing at home. (*Frank Leslie's*; April 24, 1875; J. N. Hyde.)

THE LUNCHROOM AT A. T. STEWART'S, 1875 (Top). Female employees of A. T. Stewart's have their lunch in the store's lunchroom. (*Frank Leslie's*; April 24, 1875.) MACY'S CHRISTMAS WINDOW, 1884 (Bottom). A crowd gathers outside the show window of Macy's at the height of the Christmas shopping season in 1884, when the store was located at Sixth Avenue and 14th Street. Founded near this location ·in 1858, Macy's moved to its present site in Herald Square in 1902, where it carries on the tradition of spectacularly decorated windows during the Christmas season. (*Frank Leslie's*; December 20, 1884.)

CHRISTMAS SHOPPING ON GRAND STREET, 1890 (Above). Grand Street remained one of the city's leading shopping centers through the 1920s. (*Frank Leslie's*; December 20, 1890; Hal Hurst.) THE AMERICAN TELEGRAPH CO., 1866 (Opposite, Top). The Atlantic Cable went into successful operation in the summer of 1866. Though it did not always work perfectly, *Harper's* wrote with wonder of the long-awaited time, now at hand, when news to and from Europe would be transmitted and received in hours instead of weeks; when the previous day's happenings in London and Paris would be in New York's morning newspapers. This was the office of the American Telegraph Company at Broadway and Liberty Street from which cables could be sent for about one dollar a letter—a service significantly less expensive today than it was a century ago. (*Harper's Weekly*; August 18, 1866.) SHIPBUILDING, 1866 (Opposite, Bottom). Throughout the century New York retained its primacy among American cities in shipbuilding. Here a huge iron cylinder for a steamship engine is being cast at the Etna Iron Works. (*Harper's Weekly*; February 3, 1866; A. R. Waud.)

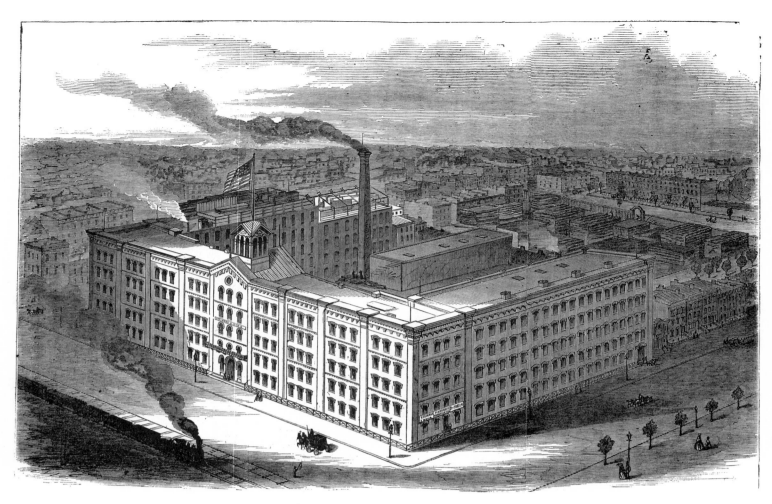

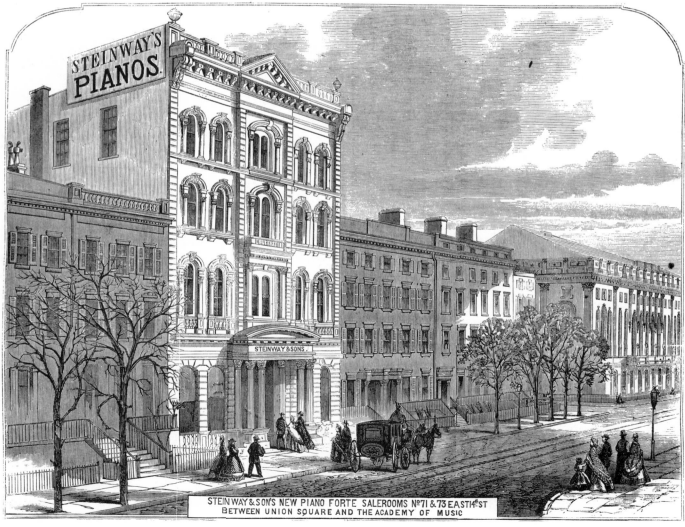

STEINWAY & SON'S NEW PIANO FORTE SALEROOMS N° 71 & 73 EAST 14ᵗʰ ST
BETWEEN UNION SQUARE AND THE ACADEMY OF MUSIC

STEINWAY & SONS, 1864 (Opposite). Two views of the buildings of Steinway & Sons, the country's leading manufacturer of pianos. At top, at the factory and lumber yard on Fourth Avenue between 52nd and 53rd Streets (beside the railroad tracks) at any one time almost 800 pianos were in the process of construction, about 45 new ones being finished every week. Below is Steinway's new salesrooms, designed by architect John Kellum, on East 14th Street. The Academy of Music is in the distance, farther down 14th Street. (*Frank Leslie's*; May 28, 1864.) SINGER'S SEWING MACHINE FACTORY, 1853 (Above). This engraving of the I. M. Singer & Co. sewing machine factory at Centre and Elm Streets was made only a few years after Singer, an itinerant actor, cabinetmaker and inventor from Troy, New York, had borrowed $40 to make his first sewing machine, thereby launching one of the many meteoric business careers which transformed the commercial life of New York and the country in the nineteenth century. The increasing sophistication of American business is exemplified by the rapid rise of Singer's from a one-man operation to a complex organization; the steam-powered equipment pictured here employed 100 men in making the sewing machines which were then finished and packaged in rooms over the company's business offices in Broadway. A separate plant manufactured needles for the machines while another factory in Massachusetts made the silk thread used by them. (*Illustrated News*; July 23, 1853.)

THE *TRIBUNE* BUILDING, 1875. The *Tribune*, established in 1841 by Horace Greeley and afterwards run by Whitelaw Reid, was the city's and the nation's leading organ of Republican opinion. This view of the new *Tribune* building at Nassau and Spruce Streets facing Printing House Square was published as the building neared completion. With a spire rising 260 feet above street level (only slightly shorter than the spire of Trinity Church) the building was one of the tallest structures in the city. (*Frank Leslie's*; May 1, 1875.)

THE NEW BUILDING OF THE *NEW YORK TIMES*, 1888. A busy daytime scene in Printing House Square, as the open space surrounded by newspaper offices at the intersection of Park Row, Nassau and Spruce Streets came to be called in the second half of the century. This view is looking south, with the newly completed *New York Times* building at the center, the *Sun* and *Tribune* buildings on the left and a corner of the neoclassical portico of the city's Hall of Records on the right. The statue seen here in the center of the square is, fittingly, Ernst Plassmann's bronze likeness of Benjamin Franklin, dedicated in 1872. This was the second *Times* building to occupy the site, the earlier, smaller one having been built there in 1857–58, just a few years after Henry J. Raymond and George Jones had founded the paper. By the end of the Civil War the *Times* was the largest daily paper in the United States; by the end of the 1880s the first building was inadequate for the newspaper whose leadership in the field, especially following its work in exposing the Tweed Ring, was unchallenged. The construction of this second *Times* building was one of the engineering miracles of the age. Builder David H. King, Jr., who earlier had erected the pedestal of the Statue of Liberty, was able to construct architect George B. Post's design around the older building without forcing the newspaper to vacate the premises or miss a single day of publication. New foundations were dug, walls, floors and ornaments went up, and unneeded pieces of the older building came down simultaneously, without incident and with amazing speed for so big a job. The result, a striking commercial building in the Romanesque Revival style, was considered one of the handsomest of its kind in the city. However, the new building was not the *Times'* home for long; in the first decade of the twentieth century the paper moved to new quarters in another striking new building, at 42nd Street. (*Harper's Weekly*; October 27, 1888; Charles Graham.)

WALL STREET, 1866. Wall Street, looking west toward Trinity Church on Broadway. This was the third Episcopal church to stand on this historic site. Designed by Richard Upjohn in the Gothic Revival style, it was completed in 1846 and still stands, now dwarfed by the steel-and-glass towers of the financial district. The pillared building on the left, opened as the Merchants Exchange in 1842, served as the Customs House in the 1860s. Enlarged by McKim, Mead and White, it still stands. (*Harper's Weekly*; June 23, 1866; from a photograph by William B. Austin.)

THE GOLD ROOM, 1869. The Gold Room, where gold was bought
and sold, was often the scene of frantic activity in the financial
district. (*Harper's Weekly*; September 24, 1869.)

BROAD STREET DURING THE PANIC, 1873 (Above). The Panic of 1873 was brought on by overspeculation in railroad securities and a general overexpansion among the country's leading financial institutions. The immediate cause of the Panic in New York City was the unforseen collapse of the Jay Cooke & Co. bank on September 18, followed by many other bankruptcies among Wall Street firms. The depression following the Panic lasted for several years and saw half a million workers unemployed and increasing strength among radical elements in American labor organizations. This view of Broad Street, looking south from Wall Street, was no doubt taken from the steps of the Sub-Treasury Building on the northeast corner of Wall and Nassau Streets. The unimposing facade of the New York Stock Exchange is on the east side of Broad Street, the fourth building from the corner. The present Exchange, a more imposing

building built in 1901–03, occupies the same site. The Drexel Building, headquarters of J. P. Morgan & Co., is at the far left, on the west side of Broad Street. (*Harper's Weekly*; October 11, 1873; from a photograph by Rockwood.) THE NEW YORK STOCK EXCHANGE, 1881 (Opposite). The bustling Board Room of the New York Stock Exchange, the center of the nation's financial capital. When this view was drawn, the Exchange building on Broad Street, opened in 1865, had just been enlarged under the direction of architect James Renwick. The membership of the Exchange—400 in 1865—had increased to 1100 (and the price of a seat had gone from $3000 to $34,000). To handle the increased activity the directors of the Exchange had bought adjacent property on Broad and New Streets and remodeled the building to incorporate the new space. (*Harper's Weekly*; September 10, 1881; Graham & Thulstrup.)

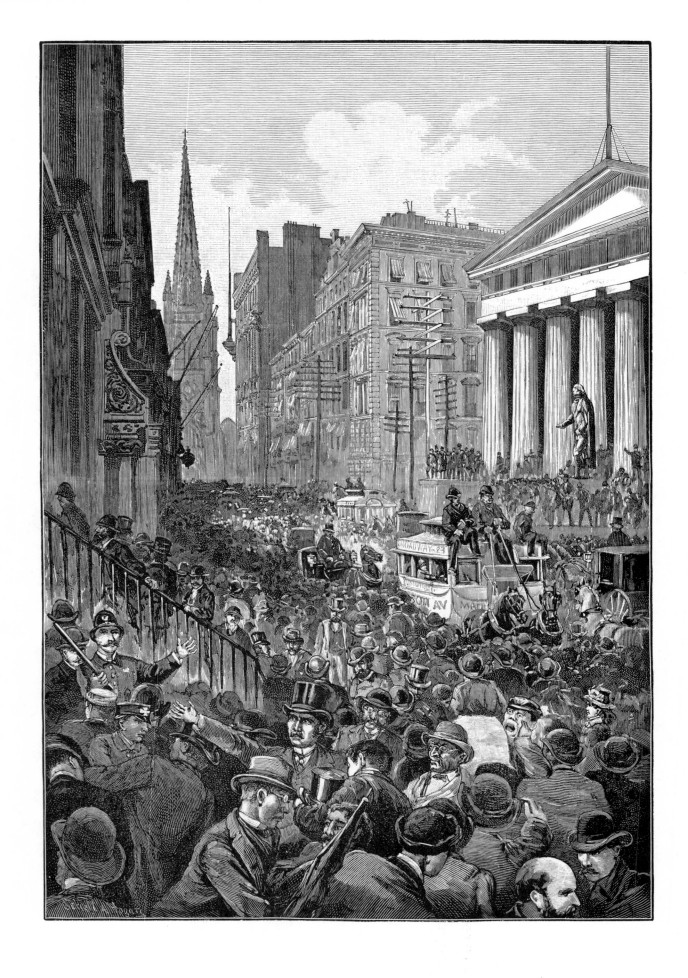

WALL STREET DURING THE PANIC OF 1884. Wall Street, looking west toward Trinity Church past the Washington statue on the steps of the Sub-Treasury building on May 14, 1884, when a brief panic was caused by the sudden failure of the Grant and Wood Bank. Despite the flurry of unusual activity, the Panic was not as serious in its consequences as earlier panics had been and business soon returned to normal. (*Harper's Weekly*; May 24, 1884; Schell & Hogan.)

THE TOWER FROM THE HOUSE TOPS.

PRODUCE EXCHANGE, 1884. One of the most striking new features of lower Manhattan toward the end of the century was the new Produce Exchange building, designed by George B. Post and completed in 1884 at Bowling Green on Beaver Street. The huge red-brick structure with its high square tower dominated the skyline for decades before it was demolished in 1957. (*Harper's Weekly*; May 3, 1884; Schell & Hogan.)

THE CLEARING HOUSE, 1887 (Opposite, Top). A crowded scene in the rooms of the New York Clearing House Association in a building at Nassau and Pine Streets. The New York Clearing House Association was first organized in the 1850s; in addition to its routine function of resolving daily each bank's financial position with respect to all the others, it provided a forum for the banks to act together during periods of financial crisis. The frequent panics of the 19th century gave it many opportunities. Every day representatives of New York's banks assembled in this room to clear their respective debits and credits on each other's accounts. Thousands of transactions, often involving hundreds of millions of dollars, were thus carried out each day by expert clerks in an incredibly short time—a far cry from the days when each bank had to send representatives to every other bank to which it owed money or by which it was owed money. Under the Clearing House's method of operation, once each bank's debits and credits were tallied, it only remained for those banks owing money on balance to deposit the amount it owed with the Clearing House where it was distributed to the appropriate banks. This was carried out by the close of the business day; the process

began again the following morning. (*Harper's Weekly*; August 27, 1887.) DIVIDEND DAY AT THE BOWERY SAVINGS BANK, 1870 (Opposite, Bottom). Twice a year savings bank depositors lined up to receive their interest, the lines often extending out the main door and up the street. Having opened this office near Grand Street in 1834, The Bowery was by this time the largest savings bank in the United States, with over $20 million on deposit (an average of $385 per depositor). (*Harper's Weekly*; July 23, 1870.) THE SUB-TREASURY BUILDING, 1881 (Above). A view inside the turret on the roof of the Sub-Treasury Building in 1881 shows the recently installed complement of Gatling guns deployed to cover any possible approach to the building from neighboring streets or rooftops. The guns were not installed in the Sub-Treasury because of fear of simple bank robbers or master criminals; what the government feared was a mob attack against the Treasury Department's fortress in search of the millions in gold, silver and paper money which was usually to be found there. Perhaps only 18 years after the Draft Riots such a fear did not seem so unreasonable. (*Frank Leslie's*; April 9, 1881.)

TEA TASTING IN A FRONT STREET WAREHOUSE, 1876. In a Front Street warehouse a group of highly-skilled professional tea tasters sample the quality of a recent shipment. The importation of tea into America, depressed during the Civil War, had skyrocketed as soon as peace returned. 59 million pounds of tea were imported in 1875 (almost triple the total for 1862) after import duties had been removed. (*Frank Leslie's*; February 2, 1876.)

NEW YORK CENTRAL GRAIN ELEVATOR, 1877. The grain elevator of the New York Central and Hudson River Railroad stood on the Hudson River at the foot of 60th Street where it received grain brought by rail from the interior and transferred it to ships for markets up and down the coast and around the world. The cutaway at one end shows its huge capacity (it could hold well over a million bushels). The building, 380 feet long and 150 feet high, did its work with steam-powered equipment on a scale and with a degree of efficiency which seemed fantastic to the older generation of the city's grain merchants who could easily recall a day when all of this had been done by hand. (*Harper's Weekly*, December 22, 1877; drawn by W. P. Snyder from a sketch by Theodore R. Davis.)

TROPICAL FRUITS AT BURLING SLIP, 1870 (Top). While the masts of ships of all nations crowd the docks, many varieties of tropical fruit just landed from the Caribbean and South America are being sold and carted away in the foreground. (*Harper's Weekly*; June 18, 1870; A. R. Waud.) ALONG THE DOCKS, 1871 (Bottom). The West Side waterfront on Cortlandt Street (here misspelled above a restaurant door) on a winter night. These little restaurants, called coffee-booths, abounded along the docks in the second half of the nineteenth century. Here a policeman tells a woman with her child to move along; a newsboy and a coatless girl stare enviously at the door, lacking the few cents that would buy a meal; a warmly dressed man ambles on his way. (*Harper's Weekly*; February 11, 1871; G. Reynolds.)

THE WEST SIDE WATERFRONT, 1869. This crowded view of the Hudson River docks, looking north on West Street from Rector Street, shows the busy life of the New York waterfront in the years just after the Civil War. The river is full of ships of all descriptions while along the piers are side-wheel steamers and sailing ships bound for destinations up and down the Atlantic coast. (*Harper's Weekly*; September 4, 1869; A. R. Waud.)

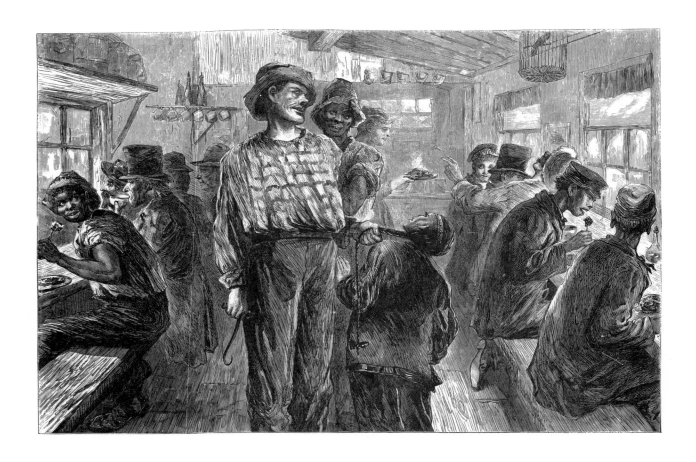

RESTAURANT ON THE DOCKS, 1871 (Top). *Harper's* reported that among sources of the soups and stews served at dockside restaurants were the city's great restaurants uptown which disposed of uneaten portions of the dishes served to their more fashionable clientele by selling them to these less grand establishments. The cost of a meal along the docks in 1871 was ten to fifteen cents. (*Harper's* *Weekly*; October 21, 1871; Sol Eytinge, Jr.) PREACHING ON THE DOCKS, 1871 (Bottom). A missionary preaches to a crowd, a common sight along the waterfront. In the background is a sailing ship bound for Charleston and Galveston; on the right one of the many oyster stands that filled the waterfront. (*Harper's Weekly*; October 21, 1871; C. S. Reinhart.)

THE FLOUR DOCKS, 1873 (Top). In 1872 three million barrels of flour and 75 million bushels of grain passed through New York's harbor, roughly half for shipment abroad. During the height of the season in the fall, the Erie and New York Central Railroads unloaded several thousand barrels a day on the New York docks. Coenties Slip, on the East River waterfront at South Street, was the center of the flour-shipping industry in America at this time. A barge which has brought its cargo of flour from the Jersey City rail terminal is being unloaded while another waits its turn. On the left, skilled inspectors employed by the buyers bore holes into the flour barrels to test and grade quality while on the right a "plugger" fills the holes left by the inspectors. A group of poor women wait to carry away any flour that might be spilled. (*Harper's Weekly*; November 15, 1873; C. A. Keetels.) LOADING GRAIN, 1873 (Bottom). While flour reached New York by rail, grain was brought to New York primarily by boat. Here grain for foreign shipment is transferred from a canal boat to an ocean steamer by means of a mechanized elevator. (*Harper's Weekly*; November 15, 1873; C. A. Keetels.)

STEVEDORES UNLOADING A SHIP, 1877. (*Harper's Weekly*; July 14, 1877; Ivan Pranishnikoff.)

SHIPPING CATTLE FROM NEW YORK, 1879. In 1879 more than
41,000 head of cattle were sent abroad, most to England, and primarily
through the port of New York. (*Harper's Weekly*; September 27,
1879; Ivan Pranishnikoff.)

CUSTOMS EXAMINATION, 1879 (Above). The vogue of European travel grew steadily throughout the century. Here a group of elegant New Yorkers are having their baggage examined for duty-bearing items by customs officials on the wharf of a steamship line. The vivid view captures the confusion and chaos of a scene with which travelers are still familiar, as well as typical reactions of examiners and examinees. (*Harper's Weekly*; March 29, 1879; Ivan Pranishnikoff.) LONGSHOREMEN WAITING FOR A JOB, 1881 (Opposite, Top). A group of longshoremen on South Street wait for jobs.

The cargo hook in the belt of the man on the right is a piece of equipment that hasn't changed in over a century. (*Harper's Weekly*; August 13, 1881.) CANAL BOATS AT COENTIES SLIP, 1884 (Opposite, Bottom). A colony of canal boats tied up at Coenties Slip for the winter, when the inland canals were closed because of ice. The boatmen often lived with their families for the entire winter aboard their small craft, waiting for the return of warmer weather and the resumption of their journeys to the interior. (*Harper's Weekly*; February 16, 1884; E. J. Meeker.)

LAUNCHING THE *MAINE*, 1890. Fifteen thousand New Yorkers and a host of dignitaries assembled at the Brooklyn Navy Yard in November, 1890 to watch the launching of the Navy's new armored cruiser, the *Maine*, the largest ship built in the Western Hemisphere up to that time. No one could have predicted that the mammoth, seemingly indestructible ship would be blown up and sunk in Havana's harbor eight years later, sparking the Spanish-American War. (*Harper's Weekly*, November 29, 1890; J. O. Davidson.)

ARRIVAL OF THE *GREAT EASTERN*, 1860. Always curious and enthusiastic about new developments in science and technology, New Yorkers turned out in great numbers to greet the largest ship in the world, England's *Great Eastern* (seen here from Staten Island—a corner of Fort Tompkins is in the lower left) as she entered New York Harbor completing her first crossing on June 28, 1860. There was some concern over whether the 680-foot side-wheel steamer of 22,500 tons, built completely of iron, would go aground off Sandy Hook, but after some rearranging of the cargo the channel proved just deep enough and the landing was successful. The *Great Eastern's* greatest accomplishment was the laying of the successful 1866 Atlantic Cable, a task for which her size made her well suited. With a crew of 400 and a capacity of 4000 passengers, she was a ship ahead of her time. She proved too costly to run as a passenger and cargo ship on the Atlantic and was broken up in 1887. Not until 1899 was a larger ship built. (*Harper's Weekly*; July 7, 1860.)

THE EAST RIVER ICE BRIDGE, 1871 (Top). Twice in the early months of 1871 an ice bridge was formed when ice was pushed up the river at high tide. Each time it only lasted about four hours; it broke up again at low tide. All who were caught on the ice as it started to break up had to be rescued by tugs and ferries as they floated toward the bay on rafts of ice. (*Harper's Weekly*; March 4, 1871; Theodore R. Davis.) THE ICE BLOCKADE, 1875 (Bottom). The first months of 1875 saw the coldest winter in memory up and down the Atlantic coast, marked by unusual ice conditions in New York's harbor. There were many rescue scenes like this one, when New Yorkers, caught on the ice bridge as it broke up, had to be rescued by tugs. Fortunately, no lives were reported lost. (*Harper's Weekly*; March 13, 1875; Schell & Hogan.)

NEW YORK HARBOR, 1873. Ferries, barges, tugboats, sailing ships and side-wheel steamers fill the harbor and the East River waterfront in this view (with Governor's Island on the far left) drawn from the Brooklyn tower of the great bridge as it was under construction. Across the river the Manhattan tower is seen at a similar stage. At this time, before the skyscraper age, the tallest structure seen on Manhattan is still the spire of Trinity Church (right center). Within a few decades, Trinity was dwarfed by the steel towers of the financial district. (*Harper's Weekly*, November 1, 1873; C. E. H. Bonwill.)

DEMOLITION OF FLOOD ROCK, 1885 (Top). Fifty thousand New Yorkers assembled along both sides of the East River in October, 1885 to witness what *Harper's* proudly described as "the greatest single discharge of explosive material that has ever been produced by human agency." The center of attention was Flood Rock, an island and reef in the Hell Gate whose removal was needed for the safe passage of larger shipping through the channel. Everything went off as planned though *Harper's* man on the scene went away somewhat disappointed that the effects of the blast were not more spectacular. This view of the great ex-

plosion is from 87th Street on the Manhattan side. (*Harper's Weekly;* October 17, 1885; Charles Graham.) DREDGING THE HARBOR, 1882 (Bottom). A dredging scow at work in New York harbor, as drawn for *Harper's* by artist John Henry Twacthman during one of the painter's visits through New York at a time in his active career when he was primarily painting in Europe. Dredges such as this were used both to deepen channels for ocean-going craft and, more often, to salvage cargo from ships that had sunk in the harbor, often as a result of fire on board. (*Harper's Weekly;* June 10, 1882; J. H. Twacthman.)

A TOW AT THE BATTERY, 1884. A tugboat pulls a procession of barges past the lower Manhattan waterfront. The massive form of the Produce Exchange building matches the spire of Trinity Church as the tallest structures on the skyline. The oval shape of the ferryboat seen close to the shore is very much like the ferries still in use today between Manhattan and Staten Island. (*Frank Leslie's*; September 27, 1884.)

THE NAVAL PARADE, 1889 (Top). An elegant group on the roof of the Washington Building at the foot of Broadway watches the huge naval parade on April 29 which was part of the city's three-day celebration of the centennial of George Washington's first inauguration as President of the United States. Spectators line the waterfront as hundreds of boats and ships of all descriptions fill the harbor from Castle Williams on Governor's Island (left) to well beyond the Statue of Liberty (right). The fleet was led by the U.S.S. *Despatch* (the largest ship on the direct line between Castle Williams and Battery Park) which carried the newly-elected President, Benjamin Harrison. Castle Garden is directly below the Washington Building; within a few years, it would be converted from the city's immigration depot into the Aquarium. The elevated railroad tracks were a fairly recent addition to this, the oldest of New York's neighborhoods. *Harper's Weekly*; May 11, 1889; Charles Graham.) THE SINKING OF THE *OREGON*, 1886 (Opposite, Bottom). One of the most most memorable shipping disasters to occur near New York's harbor took place on March 14, 1886 off Fire Island when the 7500-ton steamer *Oregon*, bound for New York, was rammed at the water line off her port bow just before daybreak by a schooner which tore a huge hole in the steamer's hull and then disap-

peared without a trace. Efforts to close the hole and pump out the inrushing water failed; guns and rockets were fired off to attract help and under the direction of Captain Philip Cottier the evacuation of the Cunard Line steamer took place smoothly. Some crew members tried to rush the lifeboats, but were held off by the ship's officers. The New York pilot ship *Phantom* arrived on the scene and, with another small craft which answered the call, successfully transferred all 896 passengers and crew members of the *Oregon* to the German steamer *Fulda,* also bound for the city, which had come across the scene of the accident a few hours after the collision. Eight hours and fifteen minutes after the collision, the *Oregon* sank with great loss of property but with no loss of life, except for the passengers aboard the schooner which had rammed her. The *Oregon* had been built only three years before at a cost of a million dollars; she had briefly been the fastest Atlantic steamer, having made the run from Queenstown, Ireland to Sandy Hook in six days, nine hours and twenty-two minutes. This view, which shows the *Oregon* on the right, the *Phantom* on the left and the *Fulda* in the center was drawn from accounts furnished by the officers of the *Oregon*. *Harper's Weekly*; March 27, 1886; Schell & Hogan.)

THE WESTFIELD EXPLOSION, 1871 (Left). One of the worst disasters ever to occur along New York's waterfront took place on July 30, 1871 when the boiler of the Staten Island ferry *Westfield* exploded as the boat was getting ready to leave her slip at the foot of Whitehall Street. Passengers and crew were hurled into the air, scalded with steam and boiling water from the boiler and pinned under sections of the boat blown loose by the explosion. About 100 of the 400 persons on board were killed. The sketch for this engraving was made from the deck of the *Westfield's* sister ship *Northfield*, which drew up immediately afterward to take off survivors and the bodies of the dead. *Harper's* reported that the boat's pilot-house, with the pilot in it, was catapulted straight up into the air by the explosion, crashed back upon the deck and splintered in pieces, but the pilot, to his own amazement, walked away unhurt. (*Harper's Weekly*; August 12, 1871; W. Long Palin.) EVACUATION DAY MARINE PARADE, 1883 (Below). On a rainy November

25, 1883, *Harper's* artist Charles Graham climbed to the Brooklyn tower of the bridge, opened only six months earlier, to sketch this marine parade (similar to Operation Sail of 1976) marking the centennial of Evacuation Day, the day when British troops left New York near the end of the American Revolution. The few taller buildings built in Lower Manhattan begin to rival the church spires as the city's tallest structures. (*Harper's Weekly*; December 8, 1883; Charles Graham.) THE FERRY BELL, 1873 (Right). A fog-bell ringer guides a ferryboat into its pier at the foot of Roosevelt Street on the East Side waterfront. The bells at the end of each pier were struck a different number of strokes for the different ferries, of which there were a great number at this time, helping the skilled captains to find the right pier even in the densest fog, although once away from the piers the dangers of collision between boats of different lines was still great. (*Harper's Weekly*; February 8, 1873; E. A. Abbey.)

STREETCAR BLOCKADE, 1871 (Top). A scene in The Bowery as a heavy snowstorm brought the horse-drawn streetcar lines to a total halt. (*Harper's Weekly*; March 3, 1871; Stanley Fox.) CLEARING STREETCAR TRACKS, 1877 (Bottom). The congestion and confusion caused on the city's streets by a heavy snowfall is vividly illustrated in this engraving depicting the effects of a storm. The curious vehicle in the upper left is a primitive snowplow being pulled along streetcar tracks by a team of ten horses. When this cumbersome apparatus arrived at a busy intersection, all the regular traffic was forced to a standstill. (*Harper's Weekly*; January 20, 1877; Ivan P. Pranishnikoff.)

A FIFTH AVENUE BUS, 1891. (Top). With three horses abreast, it took these coaches one hour and thirty-two minutes to make a round trip up and down the length of Fifth Avenue. The fare was ten cents each way, or for as far as you wanted to go uptown or downtown, but many people simply made the complete trip for relaxation on a summer night. The buses went out at 7:30 in the morning and ended their last run at 10:30 in the evening. (*Harper's Weekly*; July 11, 1891; C. S. Reinhart.) A RUNAWAY HORSE, 1890 (Bottom). A common hazard of nineteenth-century city life, a runaway horse, is seen here on the Brooklyn Bridge. (*Harper's Weekly*; March 15, 1890 John Durkin.)

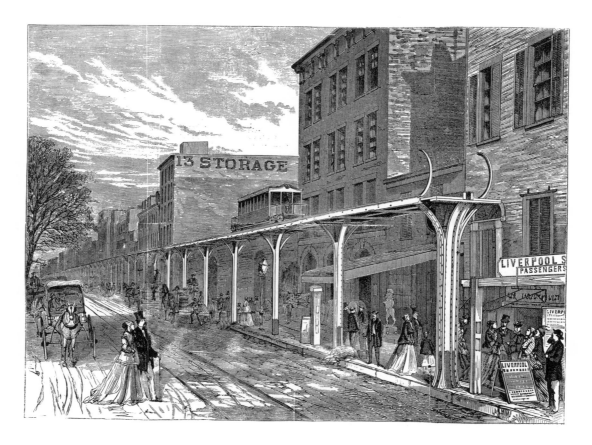

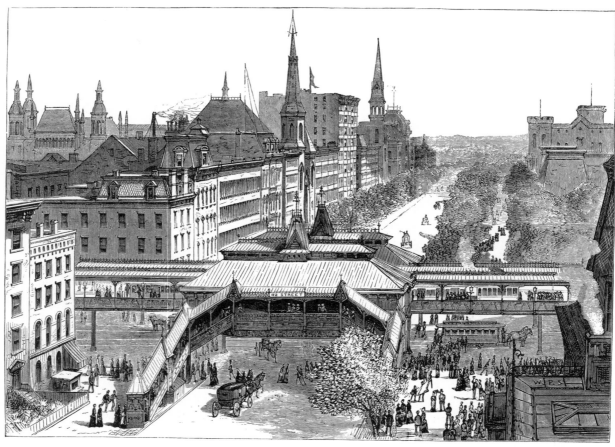

THE ELEVATED IN GREENWICH STREET, 1868 (Top). Developed by Charles T. Harvey, the city's first elevated railroad went into operation along Greenwich Street in 1868. At first the line ran only from the Battery to Cortlandt Street, but it was extended to 30th Street in 1870 and eventually as far north as 59th Street. Contemporary accounts make a point of mentioning the incredible amount of noise the elevated made. (*Harper's Weekly*; July 25, 1868; Stanley Fox.) THE SIXTH AVENUE ELEVATED, 1878 (Bottom). By 1878 an elevated railway ran along Sixth Avenue from the Battery to Central Park. In this view looking east, we see the station on tree-lined 42nd Street. At the right are the massive walls of the Croton Reservoir, where the New York Public Library now stands, while in the distance, on the north side of the street, is a portion of the mansard roof of Grand Central Terminal. (*Harper's Weekly*; July 20, 1878; W. P. Snyder.)

THE ELEVATED AT FRANKLIN SQUARE, 1878. The imposing offices of Harper & Brothers, then the largest publisher in America, stand on the left. The inset shows the Hanover Square station. (*Harper's Weekly*; September 7, 1878; Theodore R. Davis.)

GRAND CENTRAL TERMINAL, 1872. Exterior and interior views of Grand Central Terminal, at Fourth Avenue and 42nd Street, soon after the handsome, mansard-roofed structure was completed in the fall of 1871. Planned by Cornelius Vanderbilt, the new depot brought together the offices and facilities of three railroads—the New York & Harlem, the New York Central & Hudson, and the New York, New Haven & Hartford. This concentration rapidly made it one of the focal points of New York life, celebrated in both its history and literature. The exterior view is from the south side of 42nd Street while the interior shows the immense "car house" or train shed inside the station. The 80,000-square-foot glass roof of the train shed was supported by 31 iron trusses, each weighing 40 tons—so heavy that they were erected in sections by derricks on movable stages in one of the great engineering feats of the city's history. This Grand Central Terminal was enlarged and remodeled in 1899. In 1903 land rights were obtained which enabled trains to be run underground north of the station, as they are today, and the train shed was removed in 1906. In 1910 the entire station was demolished to be replaced by the present Grand Central Terminal, designed by Warren & Wetmore, which opened three years later. (*Harper's Weekly*; February 3, 1872; exterior by Stanley Fox from a photograph by C. K. Bill; interior by Fox from a photograph by Rockwood.)